Contents

KT-499-289

Acknowledgements

We should like to thank those who have helped at various stages in the preparation of the text, in particular Jo Compton, Eric Pascoe, Pat Shenstone, Beverley Smith and John Borrows who commented on the draft text, and also David Scott, Head of Business Studies, and the many GNVQ Advanced Art students of Wootton Bassett School, Wiltshire.

In addition, we would like to thank the following people who greatly assisted in providing information on progression routes: Tony Charlton, Universities and Colleges Admission Service (UCAS); Richard Stearman, Industrial Lead Body for Design; The Association for Ceramic Training and Development; The National Textile Training Group; and the Saddlery and Leathergoods Training Company.

We are grateful for the cooperation of those who have permitted us to use photographs of their businesses:

The Art Workshop, Malmesbury
Barnes & Son (Saddlers), Malmesbury
Burham Oil plc, Swindon
Cameo Print Ltd., Chippenham
Chiaroscuro Interior Design Ltd., Wootton Bassett
Graphic Image (Exhibition and Display), Chippenham
Great Western Packaging Ltd., Swindon
The Pottery, Malmesbury
Quetzel, Mexican Arts & Crafts, Chippenham
Simpson Printers Ltd., Swindon
A. E. Tunley & Son, Swindon
Westernprint Ltd., Calne
Wiltshire Signs and Engravers Ltd., Chippenham

Extracts from the GNVQ specifications are reproduced by permission of NCVQ. The material on page 26 is Crown Copyright.

Cover illustration: Mike Abbott and Kim Ellwood/Crafts Council.

Introduction

--- --- --- --- --- --- --- --- ---

Why do I need to know about business and professional practice?

People employed in art-related jobs can work at many different levels and in many different disciplines and areas, from running a large international design studio to being a freelance artist or craftworker based at home. Whatever their role, they all need to have an understanding of business and professional practices. That is why a unit about business and professional practice in the area of art, craft and design has been included in the GNVQ course.

If you are going to make a living from the work you produce – either for yourself or as an employee – or work in any capacity in the world of art, craft and design, you will need an understanding of how businesses function, together with an awareness of the opportunities and career paths available to you.

The art world is not one which is simply based in a studio. There is a vast and varied industry operating which you will need to know about and understand. How does it operate? What does it offer? Where can you find out about it? Why is it important? How do you start to investigate it?

If we look around, we see that the hand of the artist, the designer and the craftmaker is everywhere. Anything that is manufactured has to be designed – clothes, fabrics, furniture, houses, cars. All have to function. Colour, shape, form and surface pattern have to be originated and developed. Artefacts have to be manufactured and then marketed, advertised and sold. If a painting has been produced, the artist must make decisions about framing, using an agent, finding exhibition space or using a gallery. A product designer, working on a brief for a range of table lamps, has to be aware of the law on health and safety, consumer protection and copyright. He or she also has to know about market research and marketing methods. There are many things to consider.

The business and professional practice unit is therefore an integral part of the GNVQ course. The GNVQ is a *vocational* qualification. If you wish to earn most of your future income from an art, craft or design career, it will help you to decide which part of the industry you wish to join and at what level you wish to participate, whether that is being self-employed as a photographer, a glass engraver, a furniture designer, a painter, an illustrator or becoming an employee in a graphic studio or a machine operator in a printing company.

The skills you gain through studying this unit are useful in other non-art-related areas. They are transferable skills: skills which most employers want in many different areas of work and therefore will help you in whatever job you eventually choose.

How will this book help me?

The business and professional practice unit consists of three elements:

▶ Investigate business practice in art, craft and design
▶ Analyse professional responsibilities in art, craft and design
▶ Investigate progression opportunities and develop related skills.

This book is designed to help you:

▶ build up an understanding of business and professional practice
▶ use a variety of research and investigation methods structured around the elements
▶ construct your own individual evidence to satisfy the unit specifications.

It also shows you the different progression routes to art-related jobs.

Full details of the elements are given in Appendix 2 at the back of the book, together with a checklist to show how the work you do using the book will go towards your evidence for assessment.

The book is not meant to be used in isolation. It will work best if you use it to make connections between the business aspects that it covers and the practical work you produce for other parts of the GNVQ.

Three main approaches are used to assist you in making the necessary connections and links.

▶ One approach uses **industrial placement**: this might involve you in several days of work or work-shadowing in a local art, craft or design business.
▶ Another uses **business simulation**: a small business with a specific short-term target is set up, organised and operated by your own group within your school or college.
▶ The third uses individual **research methods**: collecting, collating and building information as various projects and assignments are undertaken and completed.

The three approaches can be combined in as many different ways as you find necessary and according to your own circumstances. For example, if you have good industrial placement opportunities, you should be able to include and apply many of the research methods during the placement; whereas if you do not have the opportunity of an industrial placement, you may need to use research methods to cover different parts of the elements in this unit and expand the business simulation.

How can I link other GNVQ Art & Design assignments with the business unit?

There are many connections and links that can be made with other units. The specifications link this unit with:

▶ Unit 4 Historical and contemporary contextual references
▶ Unit 6 Working to self-identified art briefs
▶ Unit 7 Working to set design briefs
▶ Unit 8 Presenting work.

For example, if you are working on an assignment with a client brief for a piece of ceramic ware in the style of an early twentieth-century ceramicist, you would make notes, reports and gather information about how an artist needs to be aware of what the client wants, how technology has changed and how this change might be reflected in the way ceramicists maintain demand for their products. This last point also links with Unit 3 Working with media, materials and technology. You might also be able to include some research which compares the different approaches needed for individually produced pieces of ceramic ware and small batch production. This holistic approach is important as it will help you to gain a real understanding of how artefacts develop from initial ideas through to the marketed product.

What scope will I have for developing linked assignments?

There are many opportunities to develop ideas and investigate the topics required by the specifications of the GNVQ. The differences between art, craft and design businesses can be discovered. The differences between primary (the product) and secondary (packaging, promoting, marketing, supplying) businesses and the differences between product and service industries provide lots of research topics. Topics do not have to be completed all at once; in fact it is almost impossible to do so. A gradual build up of research will help you to understand and know about the whole area.

All the areas for research into business and professional practice can be integrated into your investigations into art practice. They will help to clarify the career paths and opportunities that are available to you. The way forward may be into direct employment, or a course in further or higher education might offer better opportunities. You will be able to select the level which suits your own particular circumstances and ambitions. Chapter 5 gives details of possible careers and further training.

So, whether the areas under investigation are connected with historical or contemporary issues, artefacts or products, whether they are the work of painters, sculptors, photographers, film makers, ceramicists, fashion designers, jewellery makers, furniture designers, architects, illustrators, weavers, packaging designers, exhibition display designers, art therapists or art teachers, art, craft and design is not only about aesthetics, quality communication and emotion, but also about understanding basic professional and business principles and how these relate to earning an income.

First investigations into businesses in your area

Find out about product and service industries in art, craft and design in your area.

1 Make a list of at least five art, craft or design *products* made by companies or businesses in your area. Find out:

▶ the company title
▶ the product manufactured
▶ the type of business: sole trader (**ST**), freelance (**FL**), partnership (**PS**), cooperative (**CO**), limited company (**LTD**) or public limited company (**PLC**). (For definitions of these terms, see page 6.)

Record the information you have found in Table 1.

TABLE 1 Local art, craft and design production industries

	Company title	Product manufactured	Type of business
1			
2			
3			
4			
5			

2 Make a list of at least five art, craft or design *services* provided by companies or businesses in your area. Find out:

▶ the company title
▶ the service offered
▶ the type of business: nationalised company (**NC**), public corporation (**PC**), national/local government (**NLG**), charity (**CH**) or voluntary organisation (**VO**). (For definitions of these terms, see page 6.)

Record the information you have found in Table 2.

TABLE 2 Local art, craft and design service industries

	Company title	Service offered	Type of business
1			
2			
3			
4			
5			

WHAT TO DO ...

There are several ways to gather the necessary information. The following can be used as starting points.

1 A *Yellow Pages* telephone directory: use the index to generate some headings, e.g. Art & craft shops, Art galleries & dealers, Art publishers, Artists, Designers – advertising & graphic, Designers – exhibition, Designers – textile.
2 A business directory will give you similar information. The local reference library will have this.
3 The JobCentre will know most of the businesses in the area.
4 The school or college library should have some information or an index of local businesses.
5 The jobs and appointments section of the local newspaper might be helpful.
6 Go into the nearest town and list the shops in the main shopping area. Ask the shop owners/managers which art/design companies they use for posters, stationery, shop signs and display materials.

If you are working with others on this assignment at the same time, you can work together to do the research. One person asking for information on behalf of ten others is likely to be more successful than ten individuals enquiring one after the other for the same information, especially if you happen to be the tenth! . . .

Art, craft and design businesses

Sole trader One person operating a business alone, often from a studio or workshop and using outlets such as market stalls, craft fairs, trade fairs, festivals, etc. They have complete control over every aspect of the business, but bear all the risks and have unlimited liability. This means that their personal possessions are all at risk.

Freelance An individual, usually working and getting paid by commissions from a client or a company, under contract for the service provided.

Partnership Two or three people carrying on a business 'with a view to making a profit together' is called a partnership. One of the primary advantages is that each partner can provide a range of skills. It can also make it easier to raise capital as each partner can make a contribution to the financial outlay.

Cooperative A group of more than seven people can form a cooperative. Certain principles have to be observed, such as open and voluntary membership to the cooperative, equal voting rights, and distribution of profits on the basis of the individuals' participation in the business.

Private limited company A company owned by private shareholders, of which there must be a minimum of two. The shares cannot be sold to the general public. They are often run as family businesses and will have the letters Ltd in their name, e.g. Des Eyner & Son Ltd.

Public limited company As for private limited company but the shares must be offered to the public on the Stock Exchange.

Nationalised company A company controlled by central government. It is run by its own board and shareholders, but directed by government policy. The aim is to give government greater control over the economy and provide for greater public investment.

Public corporation A business enterprise set up by government charter. The Post Office, the BBC and the Docklands Development are public corporations. They have a chairperson who has been appointed by government and, together with the board of directors, has daily control of the business. The government minister has the final responsibility to Parliament, and it is the government who sets the financial targets for each corporation to reach.

Charity Usually non-profit making, but fundraising agencies have to submit, and prove, to the Charity Commissioners that the work they do and the money raised is going to benefit the public or the cause they say it will.

Voluntary organisation This involves fundraising, providing leisure activities or supporting a community project and is usually organised and run by unpaid workers.

A word of advice

Be selective in what you do.

Don't try to do everything in this book. We have deliberately given you several different approaches to the business unit and suggest a number of starting points so that you can choose what to do in order to produce the evidence you need.

Keep the aim of the unit in mind all the time. The book helps you to do that. It is written in such a way that it will allow you, as the unit specifications state, 'to develop both an understanding of business practices, and a realistic awareness of the employment opportunities available in art, craft and design'.

The book focuses on the things you are required to understand and know about:

- products produced and services provided by art, craft and design businesses
- business practices
- professional roles and work practices
- responsibilities to clients
- occupational standards and qualifications
- opportunities for training and employment.

Don't make this unit something separate. Your work should fit comfortably into the course as a whole. Use your practical work to find links between it and industry.

We hope that you will enjoy using the book and that it will help you to achieve success in the business and professional practice unit.

Comparing business practices

Effective research techniques

When you start looking at a project brief for practical work for the first time, there are many facets of it you need to investigate before you can begin to develop your ideas effectively. The same goes for the work you have to do for the business practice unit. You will need to do research. One of the most efficient ways of doing this is to make comparisons between a variety of different art and design businesses. This is called **comparative research**.

If your research is to be effective, you need to be absolutely clear about what you want to find out. Look for the simplest, easiest methods before devising more complicated ones. You will need to ask lots of questions. Be direct when formulating these as the answers that you receive, whether oral or written, will often need to be interpreted. When questions are not clear and precise, they can lead to ambiguity in the answers, and so proper comparisons cannot be made. Therefore, the simple, most direct questions will give you a better chance of finding out what you want.

There are several ways of gathering information. Interviews, questionnaires, visiting libraries and writing to professional bodies and agencies are the ones you will probably use.

Preparing for interviews and creating questionnaires

Your local area will probably provide a good starting point. Always write or make a telephone call to arrange an interview. There is no point in spending money on a bus fare to find the office closed for lunch. Have a letter of introduction prepared, asking if the person you want to interview would mind answering a few questions on the topic being investigated. Explain a little about the GNVQ course and ask if there is a time convenient to both of you for an interview to take place.

It is a good idea to prepare some questions before the interview. The interviewee will not mind if you refer to written notes during the conversation. Get a friend to help you rehearse before you go, to give you confidence. Try to anticipate follow-up questions, as this will make the interview flow more smoothly. All your questions can form the basis of a questionnaire for sending to businesses where you cannot arrange an interview, or which are not easily accessible or are outside the region where you live.

The following are sample questions which might be used when investigating business practices. They are not the only possible questions nor are they given in order of importance. You can adapt them to suit your own requirements.

Students compiling a questionnaire using a desktop publishing program

- ▶ How many people are employed by the company?
- ▶ What are the working hours? Are they the same for everyone?
- ▶ Is there any form of shift system, flexitime or part-time work?
- ▶ Is the business a production or service industry?
- ▶ What statutory health and safety regulations apply concerning the workforce, the product, the customer or client?
- ▶ Are there in-service training schemes available?
- ▶ What progression or promotion prospects are there?
- ▶ What qualifications are required for employment: A levels, GNVQs, HNDs, degrees? (Do they employ people straight from school?)
- ▶ What type of business is it (commercial, public service, voluntary)?
- ▶ What is the method of payment to employees (hourly, wages, salary)?

Hint
Do not make direct reference to rates of pay. Companies do not generally give this kind of information in an interview or questionnaire.

Remember that if you are sending out a letter and/or a questionnaire to various businesses, a phrase such as 'Thanking you in anticipation for your help' or 'Thank you for your time' should be added at the end of the letter. Including a stamped addressed envelope will create a good impression and may encourage a quicker response. It is also good professional business practice.

Other sources of information

More information and other starting points can be obtained from local libraries. Business directories give names and addresses. They include brief details of each business which will be helpful in selecting different types of businesses to give your comparative research the depth and breadth it needs.

For an even wider perspective of business practices, further information can be obtained from professional bodies and agencies. Some relevant ones are listed below. A letter from a group of you and your friends will be better received than lots of individual calls.

Arts Council
14 Great Peter Street, London SW1P 3NQ

Arts Council of Wales
Museum Place, Cardiff CF1 3NX

Scottish Arts Council
12 Manor Place, Edinburgh EH3 7DD

Crafts Council
44a Pentonville Road, Islington, London N1 9BY

Design Council
Haymarket House, 1 Oxendon Street, London SW1Y 4EE

National Artists' Association
Spitalfields, 21 Steward Street, London E1 6AJ

National Council for Voluntary Organisations
Regents Wharf, 8 All Saints Street, London N1 9RL

Chartered Society of Designers
32–38 Saffron Hill, London EC1N 8FH

Charity Commission
St Albans House, 57–60 Haymarket, London SW1Y 4QX

Companies Registration Offices
England: Companies House, 55–71 City Road, London EC1Y 1BB
Wales: Companies House, Crown Way, Cardiff CF4 3UZ
Scotland: Companies House, 37 Castle Terrace, EH1 2EB
Northern Ireland: IDB House, 64 Chichester Street, Belfast BT1 4JX

These organisations mainly deal with the needs of artists, designers and craftmakers. They may only be able to send you general information rather than respond to all your specific enquiries.

Investigating different types of businesses

In Activity 1 you have already begun to find out about:

1 different forms of ownership
2 the aims and objectives of art, craft and design businesses in your area.

Definitions of various types of businesses are given in the Introduction (see page 6). Here are some further examples to show the type of work they cover. You will begin to see which category the businesses in your area belong to.

Commercial businesses

The sole trader This could be a silversmith or jewellery maker working from his or her own studio and using craft fairs, festivals and exhibitions as outlets for selling directly to the public.

The partnership An extension of the set-up of the sole trader, but in this case two or more people operate the business. They could be different craftmakers – a glassblower, a candlemaker and a wood carver, for example – using the same premises and sharing the risks and profits equally.

The freelance designer This could be a graphic designer, specialising in technical illustration, who seeks a contract for his or her services from a wide range of prospective clients. Freelance designers are not employed by any one company but earn their income by offering a service. They often work from a home-based studio.

The cooperative This might be a large workshop area which is divided into smaller units, each having a different maker – a painter, a weaver, a printer, a potter, and so on. There may be a single selling outlet where their combined output is displayed and sold. The members of the cooperative share their combined profits and losses equally.

The limited company This is a legal entity that exists independently from its members, the shareholders. It has its own bank account and can own property. Liability for the shareholders is limited to the shares they hold and therefore their personal possessions are not at risk should the business become bankrupt.

In a private limited company the shares are owned privately and cannot be sold to the public. This type of company is frequently a family-run organisation who are very often the founders of the company and may also be the directors. They actually own the business and control it.

In a public limited company (PLC) the shares are offered on the Stock Exchange to the general public. A PLC has a board of directors who are appointed to run the business on behalf of the shareholders. There is no upper limit to the number of shareholders.

Public service businesses

Many of these are owned and run by either national or local government – for example, town or city art galleries and museum services, and local arts centres which combine exhibition space, drama and music workshops and performance areas.

Voluntary organisations

Charitable organisations Examples include OXFAM, the British Heart Foundation and Greenpeace. They are chiefly fundraising bodies. They raise funds by selling goods and/or by receiving donations which are then distributed for the benefit of specific activities.

Community arts programmes These offer opportunities for artists to work closely in a neighbourhood environment. There are projects, such as those run by the Common Ground organisation, which devise schemes to help local parish council groups and individuals to commission artwork.

Looking at GNVQ aims and objectives

The aims and objectives listed in the range of Element 5.1 are quite straightforward, but a little explanation of some of the terms in them might be useful at this stage.

Commercial

Making a profit This has to be a concern of anyone setting up in business. It is impossible to continue trading if the profit margin is not enough to give an adequate income and to allow further investment to take place.

Developing a market share This involves promoting the business by advertising, cultivating clients and customers, and developing the product to fill the market demand.

Public service

This involves, for example, the design of brochures, handouts and leaflets for distribution through libraries and other publicly owned outlets. It is also the area in which art, craft and design activities are organised and funded by the local authority. These may range from weekend courses and evening classes to artists in residence who work with local communities on projects involving, say, sculpture for a shopping centre, a mural for a hospital or a play area for children.

Voluntary

Voluntary activities are linked with many of the public services in organising fun events for children or adults, for example. These include things like helping to make and paint props and scenery for a local drama group and floats for the local carnival. Some artists undertake unpaid, voluntary work in order to become known in the area, considering this as a way of advertising their skills. They might hope that it would lead to a community arts project commission or to some other form of paid work.

activity **2** **Devise a questionnaire which will help you to discover different types of businesses, their form of ownership, and their aims an objectives.**

WHAT TO DO ...

The questionnaire should be sent to all the art, craft or design companies or businesses that were gathered for Activity 1 (page 4). A bank of questions that can be used as a starting point was given earlier in this chapter (page 9). Add more questions aimed specifically at your chosen business and base them on the range in Element 5.1 'Types of businesses' and 'Aims and objectives'.

Remember to put the questions in a logical sequence so that people answering them can see the sense of what is being asked. Allow plenty of space for longer answers and include tick boxes when a simple yes/no/maybe type of answer is needed. Use a word processor with a good graphics package to produce the design of the questionnaire. Remember this can be included as part of your key skills work in Information Technology. Before you send out the questionnaire, try it out on your friends and family to make sure that it is easy to follow. . . .

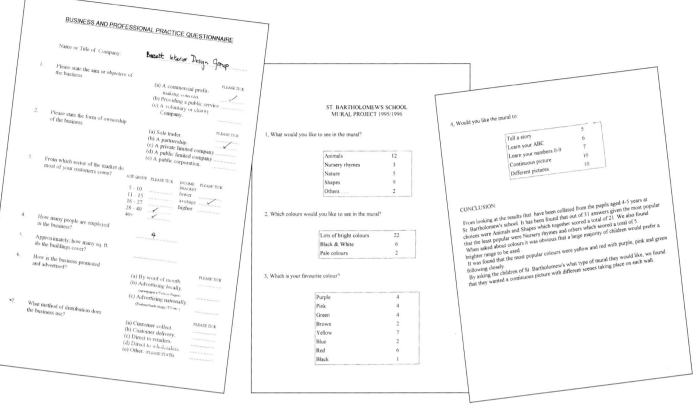

Questionnaires

Identifying business resources and demands

All types of businesses need a base from which they can operate. A business may be in a particular place because the resources needed are readily available there, or because there is a local market demand for the service or product offered, or there are financial incentives being offered by government development agencies. In the nineteenth century the right type of clay was found in the Staffordshire area of England and so several small pottery businesses sprang up. These have now developed an international market. Art galleries are often found where there are large populations or where large numbers of people visit. A little-known gallery in a small village that is not near a main road cannot be expected to thrive on just the people passing by.

Some of the best sites for smaller businesses are often where local resources and local demand are found together. Costs of raw materials, transportation, communication and delivery are much lower and so the business has a greater chance of success.

The size of the premises for the business also has to be considered. A sole trader needs smaller accommodation than a company employing a large workforce. But if the business is to develop, space for future expansion must be taken into account. The sole trader might become a partnership and then perhaps a limited company. This could mean moving to a larger site or developing the premises. Some early decisions would have to be made about all these factors, together with the amount of rates, rent, leasehold and other overheads that would have to be paid.

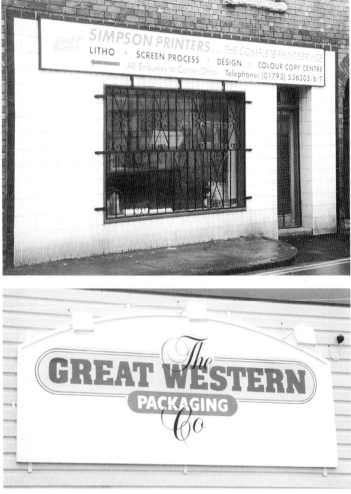

Business exteriors
(above) Small-scale craft business
(top right) Middle-scale print business
(bottom right) Large-scale design business

Some art, craft and design businesses find that the demand for their product or service comes from a specifically targeted group in society. This may be by age group. A product might be aimed at the teenage market, for example, in which case colour schemes and impact would be a dominant consideration with less emphasis on the durability of the product. Alternatively a service might be offered which is more exclusive and aimed at the 40+ age group, in which case quality and value for money would be more significant than the latest fashion craze.

Some art, craft and design businesses consider their local market as an important part of trading, whereas others concentrate entirely on national and export markets.

Today, more and more large high-street stores use a designed house style which is instantly recognisable nationally. Further afield, there are European and international markets that businesses can consider. The work of graphic designers can be seen and recognised around the world – for example, credit card signs in shop windows or the red and yellow symbol of the McDonald's fast-food outlets.

activity **3** **Investigate the business resources and facilities of a local company.**

The aim is to:

▶ **investigate why the business was established on the site**
▶ **draw a plan of the premises indicating the designated production areas (e.g. administration offices, design offices, production areas).**

WHAT TO DO ...

1 First of all, write a letter or make a telephone call explaining what you would like to do and asking for a convenient time for this to happen. Some companies may have printed information that could help you.

2 Compile some questions that will help you establish why the business is sited where it is. Questions that are linked to locally available resources and to market demands are the important ones. What are ...?, Where from ...?, How obtained ...?, Who for ...?, Which age group ...?, Where to ...? are some starting points. Add other questions that might establish how long the business has been there and how it has developed over that period of time.

3 Draw up the plan of the premises as accurately as possible. However, it may not always be possible to go round with a tape measure measuring every single dimension! Be discreet and respectful. Do not be a nuisance or get in the way. Observing these simple rules will take you much further towards obtaining useful information.

The aim is to obtain some idea of the areas that make up a business, how they function and how they are related to a pattern of working. The pattern can usually be seen whether it is a simple, one-room studio or a company with larger premises.

If it is not possible for you to visit a local art, craft or design business, a suitable alternative might be to draw up a plan of the college or school art studios, indicating the various spaces and areas for the different art, craft and design activities that take place. Many establishments have a print room, and this might make a suitable venue. . . .

activity **4** **Investigate two local art, craft or design businesses to discover how their demand has been established and fulfilled.**

To satisfy the evidence indicators in Element 5.1, your case studies should involve one *commercial* business and one *public service* or *voluntary* business.

WHAT TO DO ...

Again, write down a framework of questions that can be distributed to businesses in the form of a questionnaire. Your objective is to gain information about local, national and international demand, and the characteristics (e.g. age and socio-economic group) of the target audience. The outline at the beginning of this section provides useful information on which to base your questions. Some examples are given on the next page.

- At which age group is the product aimed?
- What factors govern how the product is shaped, coloured and decorated?
- Is the service for individual or group clients (nationally operating companies, committees, councils, etc.)?

You might ask further questions about how the initial demand has been developed in the light of either customer satisfaction or criticism and how these factors were established. This concerns market research. The next section in this chapter deals with this topic in more detail.

If the business is a large concern, you might ask other questions about the nature of its employment. For example:

- Has the workforce been either increased or decreased? When?
- Is the work seasonal? How does this affect employment?
- Are staff employed on flexihours to cope with particular circumstances, on fixed hours, or on shift work to keep machinery operating round the clock. (The ceramic industry is a good example of this.) . . .

Important terms

Financial resources The money needed to run a business, that is the capital, loans and grants initially needed to establish the business and the investment, further loans and grants necessary to maintain and develop the business.

Human resources The total workforce, from the owner or managing director to the shop-floor workers.

Physical resources The premises from which the business operates, as well as the necessary equipment and materials.

Resources of time The amount of time needed to perform various tasks and processes – for example, drying time for clay artefacts and kiln-firing time in a ceramics business. Managing time is an important consideration in a business organisation.

Socio-economic groups In market research, people are often divided into groups according to the wages or salaries they earn. Unskilled workers are put in one socio-economic group while manual and non-manual skilled workers, managerial and professional people are all classified in other, different groups.

Conducting market research

Market research is used to show the possible demand for a new product. Any business has to focus on its potential market, customers and clients to establish the likely demand. It needs to find out what the potential is for selling its product or service, and to whom it is most likely to appeal.

Many large businesses employ agencies who specialise in market research to conduct surveys for them. Small, local businesses often devise their own methods of investigating their sales potential, but all are likely to seek answers

Viewing work at a craft fair
(above) Glassblowing
(right) Jewellery and crystals

to questions which will allow them to develop short-term and long-term plans. One method used by market research agencies involves telephoning a random selection of the public and asking a set of previously prepared questions about a wide range of products and services. The answers are then collated. This information is sold to all types of businesses who need to identify general trends. The same research can also be carried out by mail shot and competitions; free gifts are sometimes offered to encourage public response. Agencies calculate the possible low percentage of questionnaires likely to be returned and counteract this by large-scale distribution. Information can also be gathered by putting enquiry forms in with product packaging and from the complaints and suggestions received by customer information services.

Smaller businesses also need to conduct surveys. These might take the form of questionnaires included in the regular mail sent to their customers or clients, such as invoices or advertising material. Other methods might include going out into the streets or shopping centres and conducting one-to-one interviews with members of the public.

Market research aims to find out about who buys or might buy the product or service, what is either liked or disliked about it, and at what price range it should be launched. The answers to these questions allow conclusions to be drawn and a business plan or strategy can then be formulated. The plan aims to match the product or service offered with the potential purchasers.

Questionnaire surveys by market research agencies

Market research interviews in a shopping centre

5 **Find out from local art, craft and design businesses whether they conduct market research and, if so, how they do it.**

WHAT TO DO ...

Select different art, craft or design businesses for your survey. Include both large and small organisations. For each business, write or make a telephone call asking if a questionnaire can be sent or, better still, if you can make an appointment to ask some questions. If you ask each business the same set of questions, you can then identify trends which are common to them all. If possible, select from both primary and secondary art, craft or design businesses.

▶ **Primary businesses** are those that are concerned directly with making or offering an art, craft or design product or service.
▶ **Secondary businesses** are those which support the primary business but are not directly involved in manufacture – for example, suppliers of art paper to a printer, or a nationwide packer and transporter of fine art.

Begin by devising a set of questions about the business's policy on market research. These questions are going to be helpful in compiling the next questionnaire in Activity 6, so if you give careful thought at this stage it will make the next activity easier. The following questions give some starting points.

▶ Do you use a national research agency to conduct your market research?
▶ Do you use your own methods of conducting market research?
▶ Do you employ anyone specifically to conduct your market research as part of your public relations or advertising teams?
▶ How reliable do you think market research is?
▶ What specific information do you expect the market research to reveal?
  For example:
  (a) who is going to buy the product or service?

(b) the earning capacity of the potential purchaser

(c) the acceptable price range for the product or service

(d) the age range of the potential purchasers.

Questions about the product could then centre around its colour, shape, size and decoration, for example. Enquiries about the service could focus on the quality and speed of delivery. General questions concerning function and materials or design quality and durability could also be added.

When the questionnaires are returned, you should be able to collate the information and discover the areas of market research which the professionals see as important. Make a note of them. They will be useful to you in the next activity. . . .

activity **6** **Carry out your own market research. Compile a questionnaire for local distribution which aims to collect public opinion on an art, craft or design product or service.**

WHAT TO DO ...

For this activity you can choose any product or service as long as it is based on the information and knowledge gained from the questionnaire in Activity 5 and developed with the addition of further questions. If you are setting up a simulated business (Chapter 2), it makes good business sense to conduct the market research on that particular product or service. Otherwise choose any product that is already on the market and produce market research for it.

Try to be objective in developing questions. What would the company want to know? Remember there will be many constraints that must be considered. For example, can the machinery that is already set up to produce the goods, cope with the extra demand or produce the new range of items? What are the economic pressures of producing the goods at competitive prices while still leaving room for a projected profit margin? What about value for money, usually a key factor for the customer or client? And what are the economic and production constraints of producing optimum quality goods or services? Having taken these considerations into account, you should then frame questions like these:

▶ Is the product a pleasing shape/a suitable colour? (tick boxes)
▶ If any changes to the colours could be made, what would you change them to? (written statement)
▶ Is the product reasonably priced? (tick boxes)
▶ Have you bought or would you buy this product? (Yes/No)
▶ If not, why not? (written statement)
▶ If you have bought this product, how long have you had it and are you likely to replace it? (written statement)

Design and arrange your questionnaire using a desktop publishing program so that it is user-friendly and aesthetically pleasing.

Once the questionnaire has been compiled, you need to go out onto the streets and start distributing it. A list of questions with short answers might be asked and the responses recorded on the spot. This means you keep possession of the form. On the other hand, if it is a long document people may need some time to fill it in. You should try to provide somewhere where they can do this. Ask the local library, church hall or a shop if the survey may be conducted there. Use a small table and chair and provide pens or pencils. Alternatively, you can set up a means of collecting completed questionnaires. A collection point or an address to which they can be returned should therefore be included on the questionnaire. Don't forget to include a line thanking people for their time. If this second method is used, you cannot expect a 100% return. People are busy and may forget to return the questionnaires.

When you receive the completed questionnaires, the information will need to be collated, analysed and presented. It should be a simple job to add up the results of 'tick box' and 'Yes/No' questions. These can then be presented in percentage form using either graphs or pie charts. A good word-processing or desktop publishing program will produce these.

The written statement answers are harder to analyse and make it difficult to predict trends and directions. However, they can be banded together into the main categories of response, while minority answers are grouped together as 'Others'. From this you can get a reasonable estimate of percentages which can be transferred into more graphs or pie charts. These give a visual, easily understood presentation, and with imagination can be transformed into a well presented document using a computer and printer to produce both screen and hard copy. This activity has components in it which will produce some of the evidence for key skills in both Application of Number and Information Technology. . . .

Responsibilities to clients

We are all consumers and customers. Every day we use products and services which we expect to work, give value for money and be safe. We are protected by legislation which provides us with statutory rights if things go wrong. Artists, craftspeople and designers who go into business, no matter what the size of the business, have to conform to that legislation. These are not only aesthetic and ethical responsibilities that have to be considered but also legal responsibilities which must be observed.

The contract

A contract is an **agreement** between two or more parties that is **legally binding**. It is often used in buying materials and services from suppliers, or for the sale of products or services to potential customers or clients. A contract contains a number of standard items, including the names of the buyer and seller, the goods or service bought and sold, the price, and the delivery date and address. The contract also binds the parties to the legislation which is designed to protect the customer or consumer.

The legislation

Sale of Goods Act 1979 Goods and services must give value for money. They must be of 'merchantable quality', match the description applied to them, and be fit for the purpose for which they are sold. A ceramic teapot that does not pour well would not conform to this standard.

Supply of Goods and Services Act 1982 This legislation covers the time taken to provide goods and services and the charges made. Its main points ensure that work is carried out with reasonable care and skill and within a reasonable time, and that the customer or client pays a reasonable charge or fee.

Trade Descriptions Acts 1968–1972 Businesses are not allowed to deliberately misrepresent goods or services in any way. This includes advertisements. Points covered by these acts include quality, fitness for purpose, methods of manufacture, and the person or company making the product or offering the service.

Consumer Protection Act 1987 A series of regulations have been made under this act which are intended to protect the consumer from death or injury. If consumers or clients come to any harm as a direct result of negligence by the manufacturer or designer, they can sue for damages.

For the specialist jeweller there is also the Hallmarking Act 1973 which ensures that pieces made exclusively in gold, silver or platinum are properly marked.

All the above legislation has been brought about to protect customers and clients, but any self-respecting artist, craftworker or designer working for themselves or as part of a business team wants to enhance their reputation and not detract from it. To achieve this, it is important to produce good quality work that is safe to use, give value for money, and trade competitively but fairly. Having a good reputation as a fair trader will give your business a firm foundation for success.

(left) A service-based company
(above) A product-based company

activity **7** **Choose two art, craft or design-based companies and explain how they conform to different parts of the regulations covering responsibilities to clients.**

You should choose your case studies from two different contexts – that is, *either* art, *or* craft, *or* design – in order to satisfy the evidence indicators in Element 5.2.

WHAT TO DO ...

For this activity it may be possible for you to survey local companies, investigating how they have to conform to various parts of the Acts outlined above. Each company might provide you with different aspects of the investigation depending on the nature of their business, but the information can be collated into a single report entitled 'Responsibilities of companies to clients of art, craft and design'.

Your report should deal with the following topics:

▶ how companies make sure the product or service gives value for money
▶ what controls are used to ensure that the product or service is of consistent quality, produced in a realistic time and offered for sale at a reasonable yet competitive price
▶ how the product or service is described and advertised within the law
▶ what safeguards are employed to ensure the product or service is safe to use. . . .

Professional codes of practice

In addition to the legislation governing the products and services that industries offer, there are also organisations and professional codes of practice which seek to influence the way business is conducted. They may, for example, hold certain political views or provide information about changing trends. This is significant to the art, craft and design area, which has three main councils giving leads and guidance to anyone working in this field. They are the Arts, Crafts and Design Councils.

The Arts Council This council received its Royal Charter in 1967. It has the status of an independent charity but is accountable to the public for its finances by way of the government. Two of the principal objectives of the Arts Council are 'to develop and improve the knowledge, understanding and practice of the arts' and 'to increase the accessibility of the arts to the public throughout Great Britain'.

The Crafts Council This council received its Royal Charter in 1979. It is a subsidising body and like other similar agencies is a registered charity. It also receives its funding from the government and is directed to support the crafts in England and Wales. To do this it operates many and varied schemes which include holding exhibitions, running an information service, publishing the bimonthly *Crafts* magazine, and organising education and training schemes. It also offers several different types of grants.

The Design Council In 1995, this council underwent a restructuring programme. Its main objectives are to be the national authority in a wide range of spheres of design; to advise and influence a broad range of design policy; to emphasise design's vital role in economic and social success; and to promote design education and training in Britain. In 1995/96 it was totally funded by grant-in-aid from the Department of Trade and Industry.

Because these three councils maintain a comprehensive overview of their respective areas, they are able to influence the industries they serve.

There are also many professional bodies which provide similar overviews and forums for different disciplines, but they do not necessarily provide legal protection or make political representation for their members. Some examples are given below.

National Artists' Association This formed in 1985. It campaigns on issues which affect the cultural and economic position of artists, helps with problems over contracts and researches codes of practice for its members.

Chartered Society of Designers This offers help and advice to designers and produces useful guides on design protection, copyright and royalty contracts.

Printmakers' Council This aims to promote the position of printmaking as an artform and assists its members by holding exhibitions and issuing a variety of publications.

All professional bodies have been formed to provide their members with a global view of their industries; they are therefore able to provide guidance as to acceptable and reasonable practice. These codes of practice are seen by everyone working in the art, craft and design professions as the ethical standards by which their industries can progress with mutual respect and understanding.

activity **8** **Either (a) use a local artist, craftworker or designer and investigate how their codes of practice influence the work they produce, or (b) compile a report about professional codes of practice in one particular art, craft or design-based industry.**

WHAT TO DO ...

For this activity it may be necessary for you to write to one of the bodies associated with the selected trade or profession. This will give you some insight into its code of practice and help you to formulate pertinent questions. For example:

▶ What are the parameters within which the professionals work?
▶ Why are they observed?
▶ Why did the codes have to be devised?
▶ Are there any sanctions that can be applied if individuals flout the code? . . .

Legal obligations

Artists, craftspeople and designers are also affected by legislation which controls the workplace and those who work there. This applies equally to the sole trader and large corporations. There are many potential dangers surrounding art, craft and design activities: solvents are dangerous if inhaled; electrical machinery poses problems if not regularly checked and maintained; certain pigments in paint are toxic; and the hazards in ceramic areas can range from dermatitis to silicosis. Parliamentary acts and regulations aim to control the use and storage of potentially hazardous materials and equipment. They *must* be observed. We look at the legislation and how it affects the art, craft and design field in more detail below.

Environmental protection

The principal legislation which deals with the workplace environment is the **Control of Substances Hazardous to Health (COSHH) Regulations 1988**. This makes it obligatory for every employer who uses (or whose employees use) hazardous substances to assess their dangers. The assessment must be recorded and made available for factory inspectors to examine at any time. It must include what the substance is, what precautions are being taken to control it and how the control is maintained. Maintaining a safe working environment often starts with the simple elements of cleanliness and tidiness. Cleaning up waste and spills properly is essential. For instance, it is illegal to pour toxic, hazardous chemicals down the sink. Getting rid of hazardous waste is controlled by the **Disposal of Poisonous Wastes Act 1972**. If a substance or process is hazardous, it must be assessed and controlled. This is carried out in numerous ways, from isolating the area and providing adequate screening, ventilation or lighting, to wearing the correct clothing and protection for the skin, hands, ears, eyes and lungs.

Health and safety

The **Health and Safety at Work Act 1974** applies to *everyone* in the workplace. Employers, employees and members of the public are all bound by the legislation. The act stipulates that employers must provide for their own safety as well as that of the people around them. The law also refers to self-employed people, which includes artists, craftworkers, designers and students in art colleges.

Machinery and electrical equipment of all types are clearly covered by the regulations of the Health and Safety at Work Act. The requirements take into account the protection, lighting and noise level of machine areas.

Materials may also be hazardous and should be used with care. For example, some paints contain arsenic, cadmium and lead. Even though they occur in extremely small quantities, it is as well to note them. Solvents can sometimes be found in the pigments used in airbrush work. Ceramics studios or workshops can be potentially hazardous. Clay produces dust containing silica, and continued exposure and inhalation of clay dust can lead to silicosis. Glazes can contain toxic substances and in their powdered state are also dangerous if inhaled. It is therefore necessary to wear a mask when making or spraying slips and glazes. It is also important to be aware of toxic vapours which can be present when lustres and enamels are being fired. Consequently these are non-smoking areas and adequate ventilation is a priority.

In many craft areas there are potential hazards and most will be regulated under the Health and Safety at Work Act. Photographers, printers, glassworkers, sculptors and weavers will all be exposed to a variety of health and safety risks – acid burns, skin irritants, cuts, etc. Therefore, providing proper first aid facilities is an essential requirement for the workplace.

Consumer protection

The **Consumer Protection Act 1987** is the main law covering the area of consumer safety. It takes as its basic principle the fact that all goods should be safe and not cause damage or injury. Part I of the act concerns the action that can be taken against the manufacturer by any individual who suffers as a result of purchasing defective goods. Goods are defined as defective if 'their safety is not such as consumers would generally be entitled to expect'. Part II makes it a criminal offence for anyone, in the course of business, to supply consumer goods that are not reasonably safe. 'Reasonably safe' means that the risk of death or personal injury must be reduced to the minimum, having regard to all the circumstances.

Specific marks are used on products to indicate that they are safe. They show that the product follows voluntary or statutory standards set by national and European Community bodies.

 CE mark All toys and recreational craft (boats) in the European Community carry this mark to show that they comply with Community Directives. This visual indication means that they can be supplied, unchallenged, anywhere in the Community. Manufacturers are responsible for ensuring this. (Eighteen Directives have so far been adopted, but only the two mentioned above are relevant to art and design businesses.)

 BSI Safety mark The product conforms to safety standards set by the British Standards Institution.

 BSI Kitemark The product meets standards set by the British Standards Institution. These could concern safety, quality or performance.

 Fire Resistance mark Furniture has passed the tests for fire resistant filling, cigarette resistant upholstery and match resistant cover fabric.

Mark of the British Electrotechnical Approvals Board The product has been tested by the BEAB and complies with relevant standards. BS3456 covers electrical goods and deals with safety and durability.

Copyright

The **Copyright, Designs and Patents Act 1988** is designed to stop 'artistic works' and 'works of artistic craftsmanship' being copied without the consent or permission of the owner of the copyright. Copyright is automatic. It comes into being with the creation of the work, which means that the maker is the first owner of the copyright. Unless there is an agreement or contract to the contrary, the copyright remains with the maker even if the work is sold. Copyright lasts for the lifetime of the creator plus a further 50 years. It is possible to sell the copyright; this has to be done in writing. Or the creator can secure a licence which allows someone else to copy the work for a stipulated period of time.

9 Select an art, craft or design business and, choosing health and safety and at least one other section, make a report on what you would do to ensure that proper legal obligations are carried out.

One way of tackling this activity would be to assume the role of either a manager in a particular business or someone self-employed working from a small studio or workshop.

WHAT TO DO ...

It may be possible for you to visit local businesses to gain information for the report. If that is the case, draft some questions before your visit. As with finance, the areas of health and safety can be sensitive. You should give a lot of care and thought to the type of questions you want to ask. It is a good rule to keep the questions non-specific. Ask how the industry *in general* has to conform to the regulations and what steps are usually taken to overcome the main problem areas.

Take note of any rules and regulations that are displayed around the workplace. They may be statutory ones that have to be displayed, but could also be specific to substances, processes or working areas for that particular company.

You should also take note of any protective clothing, masks, goggles and footwear the workforce uses. If the reason for their use is not obvious, ask why they are necessary and what the risk is.

If you cannot arrange a visit, go to your local library and complete the research by reference to books on the subject (see below). . . .

Useful resources

The books and addresses listed here will help you gain further information.

▶ *Health and Safety: Making Art and Avoiding Danger* by Tim Challis and Gary Roberts. AN Publications, 1990
▶ *Copyright: Protection, Use and Responsibilities* by Roger Miller. AN Publications, 1991
▶ Office of Fair Trading, Field House, 15–25 Bream's Buildings, London EC4A 1PR
▶ Design and Artists' Copyright Society Ltd (DACS), Parchment House, 13 Northburgh Street, London EC1V 0AH

Simulating business practices

How can I run my own business?

In practical situations, it is often more fun and more interesting to learn by having a go and getting hands-on experience. This is exactly the position when it comes to learning about the practicalities of running a business. By trying to run your own business, you will begin to understand the complexities involved – learning not only from the successes you will have, but also from the mistakes you will certainly make.

This chapter is about setting up and running a small-scale business, either as an individual project or as a group activity. It aims to give you a practical insight into the skills involved in operating a business. Making a profit or not sustaining a loss should be one of your goals, but in the context of the GNVQ course it is not a paramount consideration. More importantly, by following good, practical business practices, your knowledge and understanding will grow.

This is just one unit (Unit 5 Business and professional practice) of the GNVQ course, and should not be treated separately but as part of the whole programme. So, as far as possible, it should relate to or have direct links with other units of the course.

Look for business opportunities in the assignments you are doing. Is there a potential market for something that you can produce? If your friends say 'Someone would buy that' or 'I'd like one of those', think around it – maybe there is potential which you had not previously considered. It might not be a product that springs to mind but a service that you could provide. As ideas are generated, use a diary or notebook to write them down for future reference.

How can I organise my own business?

Whatever business you choose, the following sequence of activities will help you realise its potential.

▶ First of all, what choices do you have? Basically the choice is between a product-based or service-based business and whether to operate as a sole trader or a partnership. If you and your friends work as a group, you can cover a whole range of activities because jobs can be shared and regular meetings held to monitor progress. On the other hand, if you intend to carry out the simulation by yourself, you must consider the size of the task and the time it will take to complete. It is important not to set a target that you cannot reach. Be realistic in deciding which part of an art, craft or design business you are going to set up and the amount of work you will need to do to successfully complete the task. (Examples of possible ideas for businesses are given on pages 30–2.)

- You then need to consider the financial implications. This will have to be in consultation with the school or college art department. It does not mean that there has to be actual money involved, but you should think carefully about what you might have to spend. Use catalogues, price lists, leaflets and information from suppliers and banks as much as possible. If, eventually, you do make a profit from selling goods or services, it can be ploughed back into the school or college department funds to cover the cost of the original materials and overheads (electricity, use of machinery, and so on) and to help finance new GNVQ simulated business projects.
- You need to draw up a business plan. This should take into account the various business functions involved, including administration, accounting, production, marketing and selling. You should also consider what market research you need to carry out and how you will do it.
- You may need to order materials and check that the necessary equipment is available for the time of the production run.
- Your product or service must be matched to the potential market, customers or clients, and be developed using business practice methods.
- The product or service needs to be costed and your profit margins established.
- You should consider advertising. What type of advertising is likely to be most successful? Where is it to be placed for optimum effect?
- And finally, you have to market the goods or service.

We will now look at each of these activities in more detail.

Students running a simulated business

Developing the business venture

In Chapter 1, you investigated:

- different types of businesses and how they are resourced
- how business demands are identified and expanded
- the responsibilities to clients and to employees that have to be observed.

The information you gathered will influence how you develop your simulated business venture.

activity **10** Investigate areas which may have potential for an art, craft or design business and draw up an action plan.

Make sure you specify the following in your action plan and give reasons for your choices:

▶ **the business chosen (product or service)**
▶ **the potential market (customers or clients)**
▶ **the direct links with other units of the GNVQ Art & Design course**
▶ **the nature of the business and a realistic timescale (the general process that you will follow)**
▶ **whether you will work in partnership or as a sole trader (group or individual).**

WHAT TO DO ...

Look at the work that you have already completed or are contemplating in your other GNVQ Art & Design units. Look particularly at the following units:

Unit 3 Working with media, materials and technology
Unit 6 Working to self-identified art briefs
Unit 7 Working to set design briefs

There will almost certainly be some business potential in them. You might not find it in a whole unit; ideas might be triggered by a specific part of a unit or investigation, or by a combination of different bits of units. There are two main advantages of looking for business potential in these units. First, you will integrate this new work into the course. This is important as it will make it more worthwhile and easier to understand. Second, you will have already gained some knowledge while doing the previous work about its constraints, problems and successes, giving you an immediate and clearer insight into the potential for developing a business venture.

Arrange a time to meet with fellow course members to pool ideas and discuss business partnerships. You could have a general discussion about what products might sell or what service might be needed. You could also talk about what types of people might be targeted. Group discussion will help you consolidate your ideas or generate new possibilities. . . .

The following case studies illustrate possibilities for simulated businesses. Some are for individual projects, others for groups, and they fall into either product-based or service-based sectors.

1 **A student, with a keen interest in photography, completed a brief for Unit 7 which asked him to produce a series of black-and-white portraits to illustrate an article in a magazine. Following on from this, he decided to set up a simulated business taking group portraits of a school's sixth form, which were produced and sold to order to members of the group. This involved strict ordering of materials and time, careful accounting, subcontracting the mounting and framing, presentation, and collecting the money. He provided the service as a sole trader.**

Possible products for a simulated business

2 A group of students, some of whom had made various hand-built, thrown and cast ceramic tankards and goblets as part of Unit 3, used a series of moulds and a slip casting machine to make decorative mugs. They produced a catalogue of several designs, based on some of the experimental work they had undertaken during the progress of Unit 3, and made sets of mugs to order. This venture was a product-based partnership.

3 A student had been experimenting with plaiting clay during part of Unit 3. She put this idea forward at the group discussion because she thought it had potential, but couldn't quite see what it was. Another student had acquired a quantity of leather off-cuts from a saddler after some research into the uses of different materials. They eventually formed a partnership business called 'L for Leather', which produced plaited leather bracelets, name tags and watch straps.

4 Many ideas for businesses come from seasonal trading. Christmas time is an ideal opportunity to set up a simulated company. Christmas tree decorations were made and boxed by a group. One section of the group designed and made the decorations, while another section produced a variety of presentation gift boxes to put them in.

5 A student completed Unit 6 by concentrating on silk painting. This gave her the idea for producing individual hand-painted silk paintings that were mounted into Christmas cards. They were specifically designed so that the painting could be framed and hung after the Christmas season. The paintings took time to produce and a catalogue of designs was created early enough to ensure her clients received their orders on time. She developed the business further by adding birthday greetings and blank message cards to the range.

6 Another student, having produced a series of illustrated recipe cards for Unit 7, took the idea a stage further and produced and sold an illustrated book of favourite recipes collected from staff and friends (an instant market!). This was printed in black and white to keep the cost down and was created using a variety of computer programs.

7 One group of students, keen on graphic design, offered a service linked with a number of units. They designed and printed posters and tickets for local school functions, drama productions, discos and so on. Their services were in great demand.

There is plenty of scope for setting up simulated businesses, whether as an individual or as part of a group. The main differences between these two arrangements are that:

▶ the individual activity provides the opportunity for a wide-ranging, general look into business functions
▶ the group activity, earmarking specific jobs to group members, provides an opportunity for a more in-depth look at particular aspects of business.

Setting up the business

Having chosen your business, you now need to turn your attention to three basic resources:

▶ the premises where the business will be run
▶ the people needed to operate the business
▶ the cost of initiating the venture.

That is, the **physical**, **human** and **financial resources**. (For definitions of these terms, see page 16.)

The physical resources

These resources are universal considerations for anyone setting up in business. Although your business will be based in a school or college and therefore the problem of renting, leasing or buying premises will not occur, there are other issues that you need to take into account.

Consider your probable product or the service you are likely to be offering and their possible markets.

- ▶ Is there a practical working space where incomplete work, materials and equipment can be left over a period of time, especially if the work is large or may take some time to complete?
- ▶ Is there adequate storage space available for a few continuous weeks?
- ▶ Is the potential market close by?

The place from which you sell your products or service in this simulation is to be regarded as your premises. Personal contact can often help to cultivate customers and clients. Other students, family or even tutors could be prospective customers. If the business is to be organised on a catalogue-ordering basis (as in case study 5, page 32), you might decide to distribute the catalogues by hand or invite people into the studio where they can look through them. If the aim is a wider market, however, a more efficient delivery service would have to be used. Other possibilities might be stalls on street markets, or at fêtes, shows or exhibitions in your locality.

The human resources

You need to decide whether the business will be operated by one person or a group and recognise the implications that this raises. There are several business functions that have to be undertaken by the people working in your company. They need to be clearly understood and carried out practically and efficiently. For example, the business function of accounting requires someone in your simulation to keep a record of all financial transactions – that is, to act as an accountant. These functions and the people who undertake them form part of the human resources that are needed to run a business and are dealt with more fully later (pages 34–9).

The financial resources

Any new business must have adequate funding – some initial capital to buy the essential materials and equipment. (These are also part of the physical resources of a business.) A lot of business loans are negotiated in the high-street banks. In this simulation, however, your negotiations will probably be with your art and design faculty, specifying the cost of buying materials and how any repayment scheme from possible profits might operate. If, on the other hand, you decide to provide the capital or finance by fundraising, such as running a raffle or organising a disco, this will create a cash flow system and needs someone to account for its use. Cash flow is the amount of cash coming in (the turnover) and the cash going out (the expenditure).

activity ▌▌ **Form a discussion group to talk about physical, human and financial resources and their implications for the chosen simulated business. Make a list of all the resources that may be needed under appropriate headings.**

WHAT TO DO ...
To complete this activity successfully, you need to answer three questions:

- ▶ **Where will the business operate from?** Where will the product be made? Where will the product be sold?

▶ **How many people are going to be involved in the business?**
Groups of four or five would be the optimum number to cover the range of jobs but allow each member of the group to complete in-depth research and be fully involved in the organisation and running of the company.

▶ **How much money (real or 'on paper') will you need to set up the business?** This involves costing the materials needed for research and development and for the production run. You may have to complete this in two or more sessions, as the latter depends very much on the former. The development of the product dictates the time and the volume of materials needed to make a small batch production run. Re-orders and range development may be a further financial consideration, but you will probably make this at a later stage.

Finally, draw up a chart to focus your thoughts on organising your business (see Table 3). Consider materials, equipment, running costs, time, advertising, marketing, and research and development. Calculate their costs and include these in the chart. . . .

TABLE 3 Business resources

Probable product or service:

Physical resources		Human resources		Financial resources	
Need to consider	Possible solution(s)	Need to consider	Possible solution(s)	Need to consider	Possible solution(s)

Organising the business

Whether you are working as a sole trader or as part of a group, there are a number of business functions that you should think about:

▶ planning
▶ administration
▶ accounting
▶ production
▶ research and development
▶ marketing
▶ selling
▶ distribution.

We mentioned these earlier in relation to human resources and will look at them in more detail here.

Planning

You have already completed the first part of the planning process by analysing the human, physical and financial resources needed for the business.

Next, a schedule must be devised to determine a timescale for the venture.

▶ How long should you allow for product development before it is ready for the market? This is essential, especially if it is something that is seasonal. It has to be ready at the right time or the business opportunity will be lost. July may be the month to start planning for Christmas.

▶ When will the materials and equipment be needed?

▶ How long will it take to order and receive items from suppliers?

Other things will need planning as the business develops. Forward thinking is vital to ensure that a venture operates smoothly, particularly in a group simulation. Individual members, wanting to get on with their designated part of the business, will get frustrated if, for example, equipment or materials are not available when they are needed.

Administration

You will need to keep records. Money has to be accounted for; orders placed; goods received and checked. Anything that is important should be noted for future reference. You must also record what was done and when it was completed as evidence for the unit. This is therefore an important function.

Accounting

Accounting can be a complicated affair, but the rule is *keep it simple*. For this simulation, all you need to keep is a record of income and expenditure together with supporting paperwork as evidence. Obtain or make an accounts ledger. An example is given in Table 4. Record invoices sent out and money received (income) in the left-hand columns, and all expenses incurred (expenditure) in the right-hand columns.

TABLE 4 Accounts ledger

	Income				Expenditure	
Date	Invoice sent or cash received	Amount	Date paid	Date	Item	Amount
1 Jan	A. Brown & Sons	£27.50	7 Jan	12 Dec	Jewellery findings	£25.95
1 Jan	Town market stall	£55.00	cash	13 Dec	Equipment hire	£15.50
2 Jan	S. Ahmed	£12.65	10 Jan	14 Dec	Photocopying	£2.50
3 Jan	G. Black Ltd	£37.95	15 Jan	14 Dec	Stationery/postage	£6.45
				15 Dec	Epoxy resin glue	£2.80
				15 Dec	50 Copper blanks	£22.95

Production

This function deals with the design and manufacture of the product. It is important to monitor how long it takes to make individual items as you will need to take this into account when deciding on the selling price. Remember, shoddy workmanship is not likely to sell. Products which are well made are more likely to attract customers, give value for money, and generate further business.

(left) Making the products
(above) The finished product

Research and development

Once the general ideas for the product or service have been accepted, it is necessary to find out what the specific market for them is. This is where your market research techniques will be used.

It may also be necessary to trial different prototype versions of the product or to develop a product range. For example, you might vary the form, size, shape, material and modelled features when making candle holders. Or you could use different sizes, shapes and colours in developing a range of candles.

It will then be possible in some instances to use your prototypes as actual samples in market research. Potential customers could be shown the samples and their opinions sought and acted upon, giving you the opportunity to redevelop the product and hopefully get it right for the market. Another way of doing this, common among artists, craftworkers and designers, is to take photographs of the work and produce a catalogue which includes what the items are, their prices, what the product is made of and any other features. It could also include an order form and therefore provide an opportunity to make a sale.

A company that has already established a share of the market may have a research and development programme. Its aim would be to investigate how its market could be widened and how the product range could be expanded. It is unlikely that this business simulation will need to be taken to these lengths, but you might consider questions about expansion with your group:

▶ Should there be a bigger range of products?
▶ Is there a demand for something similar?
▶ How much more money needs to be invested?

Include your ideas in an evaluation report which summarises the whole project as part of the conclusion to the unit.

Marketing and selling

Once your product has been established through market research and practical development, it will need to be costed so that a competitive and realistic price can be charged, advertised to make potential customers aware of it and, in some cases, packaged to enhance appeal.

Costing the product

An established company or small business has to think about a whole range of items in deciding on a price for a product. Rent, rates, gas and electricity, wages and salaries, maintenance and repairs, advertising, telephone account, stationery and postage, insurance, loan interest, new equipment and material supplies all form part of the equation. These are called overheads.

If you were setting up this small simulated business as a full-time venture, you would have to give serious consideration to labour costs. One way you could do this would be to calculate the amount that you would hope to earn over a full year and divide it by the number of working weeks to give you a weekly rate. This figure could be divided further by the number of hours worked in the week to give an hourly rate.

We will concentrate on costing the product by calculating the labour costs (the time taken to produce a single item) and the material costs (the cost of the raw materials required to make it). Some theoretical charge could be added for the major overheads listed above if you need a more realistic price for the item.

For the purposes of this simulation, an easy way for you to work out a realistic hourly rate is to take the average rate for student part-time work in weekend jobs as a minimum. Here is an example.

Costing a leather bracelet A group of four students, making a range of leather bracelets for their own company 'L for Leather', decided on £3.20 each as a theoretical hourly rate. Between them they found they could produce 16 leather bracelets in an hour. The cost of the leather for one bracelet is 40p. They calculated the cost of producing one bracelet as follows:

Labour:	£12.80 (4 students × £3.20 per hour) ÷ 16	£0.80
Materials:		£0.40
Sub-total:		£1.20
Overheads:	@ 10% (advertising, utilities, etc.)	£0.12
Total cost:		**£1.32**

The cost of making a leather bracelet is £1.32. To determine the price, the students need to add a percentage to account for a profit margin and a contingency sum (to cover any unexpected emergencies).

Cost:	£1.32
Contingency fund and profit margin @ 15%:	£0.20
Final price of one leather bracelet:	**£1.52**

This is a minimum price which they can adjust to take into account market demand and variations in product range.

Advertising

A product cannot be sold unless potential customers know of its existence. You will therefore have to use some form of advertising and, whichever form you use, it will have some bearing on the profit margin and must be taken into account. It is a business expense, but targeted properly it can make the difference between profit and loss.

As art students you will no doubt have many ideas on what form the advertising should take, and your school or college will be able to provide a variety of methods for producing artwork. As a business person you must consider the best methods for getting your message across to potential customers.

▶ What type of advertising should be used? Consider both the form (notices, posters, flysheets, brochures, catalogues) and the medium (noticeboards, magazines, newspapers, local radio, television).
▶ What size and how many items of advertising material should be produced?
▶ How much does each process for producing advertising material cost?
▶ Which method is the most appropriate and economic for the product or service that is being offered?
▶ Are there any free advertising opportunities offered locally?

It is worth remembering here that the Trade Descriptions Act makes it a criminal offence to deliberately misrepresent goods or services in advertising, including quality, method of manufacture and fitness for purpose. Therefore, make sure your copy and your illustrations are honest and appropriate.

Advertisements for art, craft and design businesses

Distribution

This section will probably not affect the running of your business simulation very much. In many businesses, however, transport is needed to distribute the

goods either locally, using vans and lorries, or on a wider scale, nationally or internationally, using trucks, rail or air freight. As businesses attempt to expand their market share, success will inevitably lead to a larger distribution area and therefore due consideration has to be given to how goods can be economically dispatched to customers.

Ready to deliver

Professional responsibilities

Business functions make up the skeleton that supports the organisation of the whole business. They are dependent on each other and do not operate in isolation. Personnel who are responsible for these areas have to work as part of a team, otherwise the business cannot operate smoothly.

Designers and production managers working within the art industry have to be aware of the codes of practice operating in their branch of the industry. You must also be aware of them and how they affect your business venture.

Copyright is of particular importance. It automatically exists once the original work has been completed. Copyright is intended to protect artists, craftworkers and designers, among others, from people copying their work to the point where they could reasonably be mistaken for the original. Therefore, copying an idea for a greetings card using the same motif, style and colour scheme would be an infringement of both the copyright law and a professional design body's code of practice. Don't do it!

It is essential that your business simulation is run on similar lines to a real company.

▶ Create a company logo for your business which could then be printed on headed notepaper, advertising, packaging, assignment reports, action plans and evaluations.
▶ The administration, accounts, plans, evaluations and reports must be logged as the assignment progresses. Use a computer and a good word-processing program to maintain complete records.
▶ Take photographs to record all the stages of the assignment. This will be useful when making your own appraisal of the unit and as evidence for assessment.

The product that is being made should be of a good standard. An important part of the assessment criteria for GNVQ courses is based on the quality of the work produced. It is therefore necessary (as in the whole of the course) to produce good quality practical artwork in this business simulation. Poor workmanship and a low standard of product choice and design are not acceptable for students who wish to show their worth at this level. Your own standards and integrity should be high. Take pride in what you make and it will be reflected in the product. This will help to create a favourable impression and ultimately enhance your reputation.

This exercise should give you an insight into the teamwork and complexities involved in running a business. It is important to make a critical evaluation of both the positive and negative aspects of the work you have done. The aim is to find out in a practical way what you need to know and understand to run a business successfully. If you make a profit, that is an enjoyable bonus.

activity

12

This is a group activity. If you are working on your own as a sole trader, try to follow it as closely as possible. Amend it where necessary and include sufficient work to satisfy the evidence indicators.

1 **Within the group, decide who is going to be responsible for each of the following business functions:**

   ▶ **planning**
   ▶ **administration**
   ▶ **accountancy**
   ▶ **research and development**
   ▶ **production**
   ▶ **marketing and selling.**

2 **Each group member researches his or her designated area of responsibility and writes a report outlining the particular business function and detailing the job description and the responsibilities to be undertaken.**

3 **The word-processed report should be photocopied and issued to all other group members at the next meeting of the group.**

4 **Each group member then speaks to the meeting and answers questions about the job so that individuals understand how their work relates to the work of others in the group.**

WHAT TO DO ...

A good way to investigate your designated business function is to contact local businesses. Art, craft or design businesses would be ideal but, as many other businesses function in a similar way, they might also be able to provide some details. Most large towns and cities have business advice offices that offer help to those wishing to start off in business for themselves. They may be able to offer you some guidance. The local *Yellow Pages* telephone directory or other similar directories could provide a starting point. Look under 'Business Enterprise Agencies'.

Job descriptions are used in many organisations. Teachers and lecturers have them. The school or college might have a blank form you could look at to see how a job description is set out and the sort of information that is required. Or your parents or other family members might have a job description that you could use as a model. . . .

Producing goods and providing services

Once your business structure has been organised and the planning, market research and product or service development have been completed, the next step is to make the product or set up the service. It is quite easy to become so involved with the making or setting up process that you forget this is a business simulation. The most important thing is to establish a clearly defined time schedule and ensure that all members of the team are aware of their roles in the process.

▶ Set deadlines for completion of orders or the launch of the product or service. These must be adhered to.
▶ Advertising must go out in advance of the launch.
▶ Materials and equipment must be available when practical work is scheduled to start.
▶ Everyone in the team must take a full and active part. There can be no room for slackers or people shirking their responsibilities.
▶ Keep a diary of day-to-day activities.

Make notes about:

▶ what was done
▶ what went wrong
▶ how the problem was resolved
▶ what went smoothly and as anticipated
▶ what was spent
▶ orders received
▶ time spent on different activities
▶ coordination of team work.

You will need this information to complete the evaluation report at the end of the assignment.

activity **13** **Produce the goods (small batch of items) or provide the service for the business simulation.**

WHAT TO DO ...

The most important objective is to show the relationship between the theory of business and professional practices and a practical simulated business. Make sure the advice and instructions in the previous section are taken into account and observed. It should then be possible to show, through the product or service:

what **type of business** it is
what its **aims and objectives** are
what the **demand** for the product or service is. . . .

Making an evaluation report of your business simulation

A great deal of information will have been collected during the course of this simulation. For the purpose of assessment, it is important that all the work relevant to the evidence indicators in the element specifications is available. Group work is admissible, but individual effort should be identified.

Ordering the information

You have studied several different areas during this project. They should be categorised and put into a chronological sequence. Each one should have notes and illustrations. The following should be included in your report.

Types of business

Describe the different types of businesses there are and who operates within them: commercial (sole trader, freelance, for example); public service (local government and nationalised company); voluntary (charities, voluntary organisations). Make notes on which areas you selected for a potential business venture.

Aims and objectives

Describe the aims and objectives of businesses: commercial (making a profit); public service (providing information and involving a community); voluntary (fundraising, providing leisure activities). Make notes on which aspects you saw as important in running the simulated business.

Providing resources

Describe and define physical, human and financial resources. Show how they relate directly to your chosen simulated business. Record the decisions made at the group meetings so that individual effort is identified.

The demand for the product or service

Include a section on the market research that was carried out. Describe how the questionnaire was framed; how the survey was carried out; what the results of the survey were; and the conclusions drawn. This section should have tables, pie charts and graphs showing clearly, in a visual way, the opinions of the people surveyed. Examples are given opposite.

Business functions

Describe each business function. Report on the group meeting held to discuss the formation of the business and the allocation of individual tasks and roles. Detail your designated task and job description. Describe how the task was carried out, what problems were encountered, how they were overcome, and how that role benefited the team as a whole.

The production process

Describe either the method of production for the goods or the provision of the service. Include sections on the materials, the processes used, and how time had to be considered in the production process (for example, drying time for painted products, firing time for kilns, production starting time for seasonally-based products). Give an appraisal of the product or service, including proposals for its further development.

Advertising

Report on the discussions held to decide how the advertising campaign should be organised. Give examples of all advertising material used and, where possible, include a photograph of where the advertisement was displayed.

(a) What would you like to see in the mural?

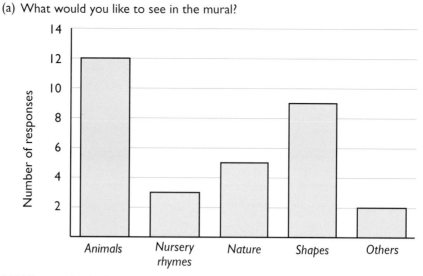

(b) What method of distribution does the business use?

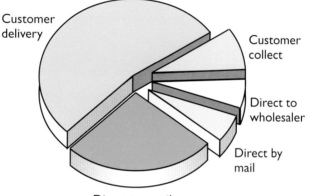

Graphs and charts showing the results of questionnaire surveys
(a) Primary children choose which topic they would prefer before the start of a mural project for a cloakroom in their school
(b) Investigating the nature of local businesses

Selling

Describe the market outlets used for the product or service. Include your catalogue or price list and, if applicable, photographs of the site showing sales being made.

Summary

Add any notes or visual material which help to draw together a conclusion for the assignment. Give an overview of the project, including an appraisal of the simulated business as a learning experience.

activity **14** **Make a display of your work. Include the product or service offered, together with reports, notes, diagrams, sketches, photographs, graphs and charts which clearly indicate the business potential, opportunity and professional practices that have been carried out.**

WHAT TO DO ...

Whichever way you decide to display the material, make it interesting and visually lively. It should have been a stimulating and enjoyable experience, so try to reflect this in the way you present your work. The presentation will provide evidence for Unit 8 Evaluate and present work.

Use a mixture of diagrams, sketches, photographs and charts. These could be interspersed with the written reports.

Use clear headings to introduce each section and set out the display so that it shows a logical and methodical progression through a trial business.

There are many ways to present the display:

▶ simple A4 ring binders
▶ flip files with clear plastic envelope pages or portfolios
▶ three-dimensional display or exhibition stands, possibly with audio-visual equipment.

Choose the most appropriate method for your product or service. . . .

Key skills

You will have used key skills in many different ways during this simulation. Do not forget to check which ones they are and to record them.

Here are some examples of where the evidence can be found.

Communication Reports, notes, job descriptions, team discussions, client consultations, questionnaires, contact with the public in the process of selling and interviewing, evaluation report.

Students selling their work

Information technology Word processing, charts, tables, graphs, desktop publishing, producing copy and images for advertising, designing logos or headed notepaper.

Application of Number Quantifying, calculating prices, costing materials, keeping accounts, working out profit margins and percentages, ordering materials, preparing graphs and charts.

Using industrial placements

What is an industrial placement?

Industrial placements can take many forms. Typically your school or college will help you to arrange a block of one or two weeks' work in an appropriate company, although on some occasions it may be possible and even advantageous for you to work for one day a week over a period of months. There are agencies in many local areas which assist schools, in particular, to organise work experience and industrial placements. Sometimes you can arrange your own work experience.

Why go into an industrial placement?

To obtain some insight into how a business operates, it is valuable to get first-hand experience in a workplace. An industrial placement could give you that experience. It is an opportunity for you to go into a company and observe the day-to-day running of business practice; to ask questions and, maybe, become more involved with some of the jobs and positions which help to make the business run efficiently.

Whereas in the simulated business of the previous chapter, a group of students operated a scheme for themselves, an industrial placement is far more about you, as an individual, being part of an organisation that is already up and running. The people you will work with have a wealth of expertise and knowledge that you can learn from and use to investigate much of the range of the unit specifications.

It is important to remember from the outset that the investigation and any actual work carried out has to be done in the context of the real business world. Second best will certainly not do. The placement has been offered through the goodwill of the company concerned. It is a privilege for you to be there. Remember, you will be working alongside people who will still be there after your placement is over. Show respect for them and the work they do, and make every effort to ensure that the smooth running of the business is not interrupted.

Getting ready for an industrial placement

In an industrial placement your investigation will be completed in real business surroundings, among the hustle and bustle of everyday working life. The research you carry out will be based on personal experience, which you will record and use to produce a written report for assessment. It will not be easy to observe and remember details unless some thought and planning about the method for collecting and recording information has taken place during the weeks before the placement.

Once you know where your placement is going to be, the first thing to do is find some general background information relating to that particular type of business.

Printing industry

▶ What substantial differences are there within the vast area of the printing industry?

▶ Can they be categorised?

▶ What work is taken on by a large printing company as opposed to a small one?

▶ What is subcontracted work?

Interior design

▶ What area is covered by the interior designer?

▶ How are markets developed?

▶ Where do they operate from?

▶ How is business usually conducted?

This background information will allow you to make comparisons and will generate further questions relating to differences you might notice on the placement. Having at least some general knowledge will also help put you at ease.

The next thing to do is to prepare questions that you can ask during the work placement. Most of these are outlined in later sections of this chapter, but if you look through the ranges of the three elements that make up this unit, they provide a list of words, descriptions and categories on which to base your questions. For example, in Element 5.1, the third performance criterion asks you to 'describe functions and resources required in business'. A list of functions is given. Two of them are research and development, and marketing. To find out about these, you could ask questions about how the company tries to develop its range of market share, or how it finds potential customers. There is a further list of resources. Human resources is one of them. Try to frame questions about the size of the company's workforce and the qualifications needed for particular jobs, or about the actual customers or clients the company has.

If you are ready with questions when you take up your work placement, you will feel more confident. You can always adapt them as you observe new or different situations when the placement begins.

Recording day-to-day events

It is essential that you keep some form of logbook or diary to record what happens day by day – that is, what work, procedures or processes you observe, *not* the current gossip! Write down any information you gain from the questions you ask. Most companies operate their own individual work schedules, so record them by filling in a chart. The examples opposite are for printing a batch of T-shirts. This can be recorded by the hour as in Table 5 or by listing the processes and procedures with the appropriate time allocation as in Table 6. Whichever way you choose, a bit of preplanning will make the task easier.

TABLE 5 **Work schedule by the hour**

JOB: Printing a batch of T-shirts

Time	Schedule
9.00–10.00 a.m.	Discuss what the job is with printshop manager Check designs Set up machines
10.00–11.00 a.m.	Print T-shirts Check quality Monitor process
11.00–12.00 noon	T-shirts ready for packaging Move to packaging bay Prepare packaging material Check packers Monitor process
12.00–12.30 p.m.	Stack and batch ready for delivery Complete paperwork for office

TABLE 6 **Work schedule by process and procedure**

JOB: Printing a batch of T-shirts

Schedule	Time
Discuss what the job is with printshop manager	15 mins
Check designs	20 mins
Set up machines	25 mins
Print T-shirts	50 mins
Check quality	10 mins
Monitor process	ongoing
Move to packaging bay	10 mins
Prepare packaging material	10 mins
Check packers	5 mins
Pack T-shirts	45 mins
Monitor process	ongoing
Stack and batch ready for delivery	10 mins
Complete paperwork for office	10 mins
TOTAL TIME:	**3 hrs 30 mins**

All the information you collect will be used in compiling the final report on business practice. Some parts of it could also be used to cover evidence for other units.

For instance, the company might have to take into consideration time constraints and their effect on deadlines; these are part of the project parameters outlined in Element 1 of Unit 6 Working to self-identified art briefs, and will therefore give you insight when dealing with your own deadlines in that unit. Check to see where your industrial placement fulfils criteria in other units. Take the opportunity to collect information and data that make links across the elements and units whenever you can.

If you have the opportunity to use more advanced technology in a placement – for example, in a graphic design studio which produces illustrations for greeting cards using the latest computer-aided design – the artwork you create could be added to the work in Unit 3 Working with media, materials and technology. It could also be used for Unit 7 Working to set design briefs, if the company allowed you time to develop your own design brief. This would help you to integrate your coursework and avoid isolating this unit from the rest of the GNVQ programme. Integration and progression are vital components in a successful GNVQ art & design course.

Using key skills

Applying investigative techniques in completing this assignment will enable you to use all the key skills thoroughly.

Communication

There will be many instances where **discussion** takes place. You will need to interview managers and working colleagues; make enquiries from a variety of sources; receive instructions; and listen and respond to general conversation face to face or on the telephone.

You will produce **written material**. This should take the form of letters, questionnaires and entries in your day-to-day diary or logbook, as well as your final report.

You will use lots of **images**. These may be sketches and diagrams illustrating aspects of the premises. A collection of photographs could help you to amplify certain written points. Or maybe a video recording might be the best way to clarify a particular process. If this is what you decide to do, ask for permission first.

There will also be cases where **reading and responding to written material** is important – for example, when you begin to investigate the background to the business area before the start of your industrial placement.

Information Technology

Your final report should be word-processed. This will provide you with the opportunity to **prepare**, **process** and **present** the information using different applications in a variety of software. The report will include statistical and graphical information, allowing you to extend the range of skills needed.

As this account will be quite comprehensive in its use of programs and software, there will be an opportunity for you to **evaluate the use of information technology**. It should be reasonably easy to justify the reason for using a computer to produce the report; compare its use with other methods and describe the particular advantages of the software used.

Application of Number

A great deal will depend on the particular type of company in which your work experience takes place. Certain areas in design-based companies expect you to employ a high degree of mathematical skills. Some craft-based businesses need basic arithmetical skills in some areas but more sophisticated numerical skills in others. Some companies are predominantly process-based and require little in the way of numeracy. Whatever the business, there will be some aspects of it that allow you to demonstrate Application of Number skills.

As part of your report, you need to produce a statistical analysis of questionnaires and draw up some scaled plans. Their accuracy relies on your ability to **collect**, **record**, **interpret and present data** systematically and use the information to **tackle problems** successfully.

Finding industrial placements

Many schools and colleges have experience in providing contact points for industrial placements. They may provide a complete support service and find places for the majority of their students. Although this saves you effort, they cannot always find places for every student in the required vocational area. You may, therefore, have to arrange your own placement, to get exactly what you want.

▶ If possible, find a placement which is suitable for your chosen career path. If you cannot do this, don't worry; whatever the placement, you are bound to learn transferable skills.
▶ Use local contacts in the art and design business community.
▶ Use the telephone to arrange interviews and visits.
▶ Plan the time that is to be spent there; it might be a single block of two weeks with one company, two separate weeks with two different companies at different times of the year, or one day a week for ten to twelve weeks.

Although this involves you in more work initially, it will help to make the time spent on the actual industrial placement both happy and successful.

You should try to select an art, craft or design business as this unit also incorporates research into career paths and further training for those disciplines. However, the choice between a primary business that deals directly with art, craft or design processes (e.g. a pottery, a graphic design studio or an artist in residence) or a secondary business that services or supports a primary business (e.g. kiln manufacturers, paper suppliers or a bronze foundry) may depend on what is available in your locality. Both will provide you with the evidence you need for the unit requirements.

Business organisation

We have already discussed business organisation in the previous two chapters. The main difference here is that the placement allows you to study a real

Work placements
(above left) in a pottery
(above) in an artists' materials shop
(bottom left) at an interior
designers, making a Roman blind

situation as opposed to a theoretical one. Once again, forethought and planning are needed to make sure that you draw as much information as possible from the location.

In this and the following section, we provide a series of activities that will help you to investigate aspects of business organisation and the responsibilities that have to be fulfilled. The amount of information you can gather will depend on the company that provides the placement. Remember that there may be areas within the business which the company classes as sensitive or confidential. When inquiring about finance, business competition and product development, for example, you will need to be tactful and understanding. Attempt as many activities as you can; any information that you cannot obtain can be supplemented by work which is completed from other activities in other chapters. There is a section about an integrated approach in Chapter 4.

Physical, human and financial resources

Businesses need a **site** from where they can operate; they need to employ **people**; and they need **capital** and **cash flow** to remain in business.

What factors control the choice of site for a business? If the business is a well established one, there may be historical reasons for this choice.

- ▸ Is it located near raw materials?
- ▸ Is it near an accessible potential market?
- ▸ Is communication easy?
- ▸ Are there good transport links?

activity **15** **Draw maps which show where the industrial placement company is sited in (a) the locality (a 50-mile radius) and (b) the neighbourhood (e.g. within the town or, if situated in the countryside, its proximity to a town or city).**

WHAT TO DO ...

The objective is to show the geographical location of the site in relation to raw materials, potential market, communication routes or transport links. Make sure that as many of these details are included as possible. It might be appropriate to relate some of these factors to a historical cause which has later led to an expansion of the business. You might come to the conclusion that the business could, in fact, operate anywhere. Write your conclusions alongside the maps. ...

activity **16** **Draw a detailed plan of the business premises. Include notes which explain the reasons for the layout and indicate the number of employees working in each area.**

WHAT TO DO ...

This plan should include not only the outline of the premises but also details of the floor spaces.

- ▸ Which room is used for what purpose?
- ▸ Where is the machinery or equipment sited?
- ▸ Where are the offices?
- ▸ Where are goods received and products dispatched?

Some small businesses operate from only one or two rooms and may be owned by a sole trader, but, whatever the size of the operation, a detailed plan can be drawn, with annotations, giving some indication of the layout and the reasons for it and showing the number of people working there. ...

You have now covered two aspects of business organisation – the physical resources (buildings and equipment) and the human resources (proprietors, managers and employees). Next come the financial resources. The majority of companies and businesses do not divulge details of their capital, loans from banks, wages and salaries and cash flow. Here are a few questions you might ask about finance:

- ▸ How do you raise capital for business enterprises?
- ▸ Are banks the only source of new finance?
- ▸ How is cash brought into the company?
  or How is income generated?
- ▸ What are the major expenses for the company?
  or How is expenditure controlled?
- ▸ What percentage of the total finances of the company goes on wages and salaries?

- Is there a target percentage aimed at covering the finances of expansion and development?
- If an emergency occurs – for example, essential equipment breaks down – how do you cover such a contingency?

Business functions

The following business functions are listed in the range of Element 5.1:

- planning
- administration
- accounting
- production
- research and development
- marketing
- selling and distribution.

It will depend largely on the type and size of the company as to whether you can obtain information about all of these functions. Sole traders devise their own schemes which allow them to cover the functions in some way. In large companies, however, the business would not operate efficiently unless qualified people were employed to perform specific functions.

activity **17** **Investigate as many of the listed business functions in your industrial placement as you can. You may discover that the company places more importance on some of them. List them in order of the company's priority and make notes about the reasons for their importance.**

WHAT TO DO ...

You need to obtain some form of job description for each of the business functions. Get permission from the person in charge to carry out this exercise. There might be forms or documents available highlighting job descriptions, but you will probably find it easier to obtain information by talking to the people who are carrying out each particular function. (Here you will be negotiating and discussing, so record this as evidence in your Communication key skills.) Don't forget that in some businesses one person may be responsible for more than one function. When you have collected all your information, sift it and organise it into a table or chart (see Table 7). ...

Professional responsibilities

This section relates to the responsibilities which are found within your industrial placement.

The business will have set aims and objectives. These will be reflected in the job descriptions that all employees have. Collectively, they show how

- the work is planned
- time is managed
- deadlines are met

TABLE 7 Business functions

Company: _____   Product or service: _____

Business function	Job description within the company	Time allocated hours per week		
		Exclusive full-time job	Exclusive part-time job	Combined task with other business function
Planning				
Administration				
Accounting				
Production				
Research & development				
Marketing				
Selling				
Distribution				

▶ ideas are originated and products, artefacts or services are created
▶ technical support is achieved
▶ communication between the workforce, colleagues, management or employer is maintained
▶ customer or client relationships are developed and maintained
▶ teamwork is encouraged and sustained.

There are a variety of roles typical to most businesses. Some of them are performed by individuals employed specifically to perform a single role, such as an accountant, secretary or designer. Some of them, especially when the company has a small workforce, become dual or combined roles. For example, a glassblower might employ a technician, but plans the business, designs and makes all the glassware and is responsible for all the marketing, selling and distribution.

You should be able to recognise the work responsibilities in your placement, no matter how small or seemingly well hidden they are. In any business involving art, craft or design, there will be creative, technical and some administrative functions. We will concentrate on these in the next investigative activity.

activity **18** **In your work placement, investigate and write a report on the following three operations: (a) a creative role; (b) a technical support role; and (c) an administrative service role.**

WHAT TO DO ...
For each of these roles, consider the following fundamental questions:

▶ What do they do?

- ▶ How do they organise it?
- ▶ How much time do they need?
- ▶ Do they perform the role by themselves or as part of a team?
- ▶ How does the team operate (regular meetings, informal discussions, etc.)?
- ▶ Do they perform one function or several functions (that is, are there overlapping roles)?

Formulate a questionnaire that can be either distributed during the placement or used in discussions with personnel. . . .

The creative role

This involves artists and designers with creative ideas and knowledge of the design processes. They may work, for example, in:

- ▶ a business which needs a surface pattern design for upholstery fabric
- ▶ a design studio that has to produce illustrations for a calendar
- ▶ a pottery which needs a new range of decorative ceramic mugs
- ▶ a fashion studio preparing designs for the new season.

Who creates the designs? Where? Who decides on the final design for production? What training and qualifications are needed?

The technical support role

This involves the personnel who operate the equipment or machinery during production, such as:

- ▶ a fabric printer producing lengths of fabric for an upholsterer
- ▶ a photographer preparing plates for calendar illustrations
- ▶ a kiln operator
- ▶ machinists making up garments for a fashion designer.

What do they do? How? What skills are needed? What training is needed?

The administrative service role

This involves the personnel employed to perform, for example:

- ▶ ordering and maintaining stock
- ▶ book-keeping tasks
- ▶ scheduling the delivery service
- ▶ publicity and marketing functions.

They include receptionists, secretaries, wages and salaries clerks, market researchers and accounts office staff.

What do they do? How does that fit into the business context? What is its importance? What training or qualifications do they need?

Formulate questions which aim to find out more about these three roles in your industrial placement company and add them to your questionnaire.

An example of a questionnaire is given opposite. Some of these questions may not be relevant to your placement, but it would not be difficult to adapt them or add more specific ones.

BUSINESS AND PROFESSIONAL PRACTICE QUESTIONNAIRE

Name or title of company: ....

1 Please state the aim or objective of the business.

		PLEASE TICK
(a) A commercial profit-making concern		....
(b) Providing a public service		....
(c) A voluntary or charity company		....

2 Please state the form of ownership of the business.

	PLEASE TICK
(a) Sole trader	....
(b) A partnership	....
(c) A private limited company	....
(d) A public limited company	....
(e) A public corporation	....

3 From which sector of the market do most of your customers come?

AGE GROUP	PLEASE TICK	INCOME BRACKET	PLEASE TICK
5–10	....	lower	....
11–15	....	average	....
16–27	....	higher	....
28–40	....		
40+	....		

4 How many people are employed in the business?   ....

5 Approximately, how many square metres do the buildings cover?   ....

6 How is the business promoted and advertised?

	PLEASE TICK
(a) By word of mouth	....
(b) Advertising locally (newspaper/Yellow Pages)	....
(c) Advertising nationally (posters/trade magazine/TV/etc.)	....

7 What method of distribution does the business use?

	PLEASE TICK
(a) Customer collect	....
(b) Customer delivery	....
(c) Direct to retailers	....
(d) Direct to wholesalers	....
(e) Other (please state):	....

8 Which three aspects of health and safety are an absolute priority?

1 ....
2 ....
3 ....

9 Who is responsible for originating or designing the product?

....
....
....

10 Are the products or services protected by copyright laws? If so, in what way?

....
....
....

11 What technical support roles are there?

1 ....
2 ....
3 ....

12 What administrative tasks have to be performed?

1 ....
2 ....
3 ....

13 What, if any, are the codes of practice used by the business (e.g. ethical responsibilities, professional practice)?

....
....
....

14 What academic or vocational qualifications are needed to start in this business?

....
....

15 What training opportunities are there for adding to basic qualifications?

....
....
....

Thank you for taking the time to complete this questionnaire. Your cooperation is greatly appreciated.

PLEASE RETURN TO:

Name: ....

Address: ....
          ....
          ....

Work-shadowing

activity **19** **Ask if you can do some work-shadowing for a day. From your notes and observations, write a report about 'A day in the life of . . .' (fill in the designated job).**

WHAT TO DO ...

Work-shadowing means that you accompany someone doing a particular job and gain insight into their responsibilities and duties. It can be an intrusive experience for the person being followed, so you need their permission. Be very tactful. Keep a low profile and don't get in the way. It is often best to complete it in a day, but, if the job is complex or time dependent, it may be better to complete the work-shadowing in smaller sections, doing a limited amount each day.

Remember, the business has to continue. Being followed by someone all day asking questions may not be comfortable or easy, especially for a sole trader.

You have two general aims in undertaking work-shadowing. The first is to gain an understanding of what the job is about, what people do and how they fit into a team.

▶ How does the job benefit the work of the business?
▶ Where does the job fit into the process of production?
▶ How long does it take to do the job?
▶ What skills are needed?

The second is to try to find out what other aspects of working there are.

▶ What is satisfying about doing the job?
▶ What training has been undertaken (either before or since the commencement of the job)?
▶ What are the prospects for the job (in terms of further training, qualifications and promotion)?

Your own observations and opinions can form part of the report, but always emphasise the positive aspects you find. Other students following on in future years may wish to use the same work placement and reporting negatively will not enhance their prospects. . . .

Legal requirements

The legal requirements that art, craft and design companies have to observe are dealt with in some detail in Chapter 1. In your work placement, you have the opportunity to see how legislation operates in practice. As there are so many different aspects of the law, with so many rules and regulations that have to be applied, it will be up to you to inquire into the legislation applying to the business you are exploring. The Health and Safety at Work Act 1974 applies to all workplaces, so this is one area that you can start investigating.

20 Investigate (a) health and safety regulations, and (b) one other statutory requirement that must be observed by your industrial placement business. Write a report on the results of your investigation.

WHAT TO DO ...

There is a great deal of legislation that covers the art, craft and design industries. You will have to pick through it to find which area applies to the company you are with. When you start your work placement, your personal manager should be able to give you some help with this.

To start you thinking, here are some of the areas where legislation will apply.

The working environment Regulations cover labelling of dangerous substances, lifting and carrying, lighting, noise, protective clothing, space, storage of materials, temperature and ventilation.

Safety with machinery and tools Regulations cover electrical hazards, cut-out switches, guards, power tools, compressed air tools, pneumatic tools and visual display units (VDUs).

Toxic materials Regulations cover acids, alkalis and solvents.

Working with specific materials Regulations cover ceramics, glass, metal, paint, photographic processes, plastics, printmaking, stone, textiles and wood.

In addition to the Health and Safety at Work Act 1974, your company is likely to be affected by the Control of Substances Hazardous to Health (COSHH) Act 1988. You could investigate both of these pieces of legislation. The objective is to find out how they are observed in the workplace and how they affect the running of the business.

It is imperative that whatever information you obtain is double-checked and approved by whoever is in charge. This legislation is complex and it is vital that you have your information absolutely correct before including it in the report. . . .

Career opportunities

One specific element of the business and professional practice unit is that of **progression routes** – either directly into a career or through continuing education. Chapter 5 deals with this subject in detail, but an industrial placement provides an ideal opportunity for you to gather first-hand information on job prospects.

The information you need focuses on the types of jobs available, progression routes that can be followed, and the qualifications needed to enter the business.

21 Investigate up to three different career opportunities offered by your industrial placement business. In particular, research the qualifications, courses and time needed to qualify for these careers.

First of all, find out what roles there are in the business:

- ▶ creating and designing
- ▶ technical
- ▶ managerial and administrative
- ▶ skilled, semi-skilled, unskilled.

Choose three different functions to investigate, including at least one that you might be interested in pursuing.

For each one, discover what is required in the way of qualifications and particular skills needed to carry out the job.

Add to this an investigation about courses leading to those qualifications. These may be full-time study, sandwich courses, day-release courses or modern apprenticeships. Find out about opportunities for employment – full-time, part-time or self-employment.

Finally, evaluate which of the career opportunities investigated might be a suitable pathway for you. . . .

Remember, before you finally leave your work placement, thank the staff for giving you the opportunity to observe or work there.

A business report

activity
22
Either (a) write a full report on what you have discovered about business and professional practices in your industrial placement, or (b) write a report, in diary form, of your own day-to-day activities during the industrial placement.

WHAT TO DO . . .
Report A
The report should be as wide-ranging as possible and should include all or most of the topics shown in the following diagram.

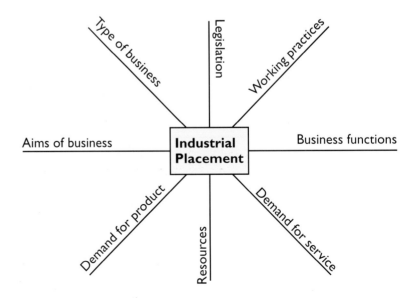

- ▶ **Types of business** sole trader, freelance artist/designer, partnership, public limited company.
- ▶ **Aims of business** commercial, public service, voluntary.
- ▶ **Resources** human (employees), physical (premises, equipment), financial.
- ▶ **Business functions** planning, administration, accounting, research and development, marketing and selling, distribution.
- ▶ **Working practices** creative origination and designing, time management, organisation, technical support, production, presentation.
- ▶ **Legislation** environmental, health and safety, copyright, consumer protection.

Report B

You will have kept a diary on what happened each day. These notes need to be organised so that you can show how they relate to some of the criteria in the business and professional practice unit. Rewrite and arrange your notes into a table (see Table 8). You could use a spreadsheet application to do this.

TABLE 8 Your activities during the industrial placement

	The activity	Chief responsibility	To whom responsible	Working practice	Where activity fits into the chain of events in the organisation
Monday a.m. p.m.					
Tuesday a.m. p.m.					
Wednesday a.m. p.m.					
Thursday a.m. p.m.					
Friday a.m. p.m.					

The following are some guidelines to help you complete the table.

- ▶ **The activity** What was the job you had to do?
- ▶ **Chief responsibility** What was the most important aspect of that job? For example:
  - making sure screens were cleaned at the end of a print run of T-shirt designs
  - that the job had to be finished in 15 minutes
  - that photographic chemicals were properly mixed and at the correct temperature prior to developing a batch of prints.
- ▶ **To whom responsible** Who was supervising you?

▶ **Working practices** Which working practice was the activity a part of – creative origination or design, business organisation, technical support, production, marketing, advertising or selling, presentation?

▶ **Where the activity fits into the chain of events in the organisation** What activities precede and follow your job? Why is it undertaken at that particular time? . . .

Consider the connections between your work placement and work in other units. You might be able to include with your report practical evidence for Unit 3 Work with media, materials and technology, Unit 6 Work to self-identified art briefs or Unit 7 Work to set design briefs, especially if, before you started the job, you had clarified a brief and sorted out what research you might want to conduct in your placement.

For example, if a student interested in fashion design found a placement in a swimwear manufacturers, he or she might have the opportunity to design an outfit using the latest in computer-aided design. This would fulfil some of the criteria needed for evidence in both Unit 7 and Unit 3. A student with a placement in a front-of-house department of a theatre might have the opportunity to design a poster or flysheet for a forthcoming production. This would count as evidence for Unit 7 and the presentation elements of Unit 8.

Finally, do not forget that your report is the work of an art student. It should reflect this in layout, in the way that it is illustrated and in the presentation. Make sketches while you are working in the placement and use these in the report. Take a series of photographs (ask permission first) which illustrate different aspects of the job and include them as well. Make the report lively and interesting to look at as well as being informative and well written.

An integrated approach

Mixing and matching: a common sense approach

Realistically, you may not always be able to gather the evidence for the whole of this unit with a single approach. You will probably collect some information from an industrial placement, some from a simulated business enterprise, and some from a theoretical investigation.

Each of these approaches, by itself, will generate a lot of evidence, but in each one you may find there are circumstances that prevent you from getting what you need. You will then have to find another way to cover that shortfall. If you use one (or even both) of the other approaches, you should be able to find the missing evidence.

For example, a student who worked in a graphic design studio for her work placement was given the task of designing and producing the annual company Christmas card. She later formed part of a team of GNVQ students who set up a simulated business designing and producing greetings cards. Because she had had little time during her work placement to acquire all the details she needed, she conducted her own theoretical research into aspects of health and safety, copyright and other legal aspects which would apply within a design-based company.

Another student had been part of a group whose simulated business involved making baking beans in ceramic containers. He had also been on an industrial placement with a potter running his own business. The student completed his unit by investigating the large-scale ceramics industry in Staffordshire.

This **multi-tasking approach** – combining theory, simulation and work experience – adds interest to the unit and allows you time to plan the integration of:

▶ the evidence you collect from the different methods used
▶ the business and professional practice unit into your assignments for other mandatory or optional units.

Completing more than one block of industrial placement

Instead of completing just one block of two weeks on an industrial placement, it might be worth considering splitting the time into two – for instance, completing two separate weeks in two different types of businesses, or completing one full week with a company and then having one day a week with another. In some circumstances it might be possible to return to the same company to work for a further week at a later time. This could be very useful. You would have the opportunity to see how the business operates and then, with permission, be able to plan a project which would incorporate work for another unit.

For example, a student who had obtained a work placement for a week in an interior design studio was able to return there several weeks later to complete a decorative Roman window blind which she had designed as part of the work for Unit 7 Work to set design briefs. Because the studio had advanced equipment, she could also produce evidence for Unit 3 Work with media, materials and technology.

Combining the industrial placement with the simulated business

It may not be possible to obtain all the evidence needed for the unit from an industrial placement. We have already mentioned that evidence about financial matters is often difficult to obtain. The business simulation would provide you with the opportunity to set up your own finances (most likely on a smaller scale) which would enable you to collect the evidence.

You might find that you have little opportunity to get 'hands on' experience in your industrial placement. In this case, you could set up a simulated business following a similar organisational structure to your industrial placement company. This would give you the chance to be involved with making a product.

Your industrial placement might consist largely of work-shadowing. You would therefore have ample opportunity to observe the procedure and detail of the job which you could then perform yourself in the business simulation.

Investigating through extended work experience, weekend work and holiday jobs

If you work well on your industrial placement and complete it to your supervisor's satisfaction, there might be a chance to continue working there for one day a week. It has been known for some employers to offer a holiday or weekend job. This would be very useful as you could collect more in-depth evidence.

Of course, weekend work and holiday jobs are not always easy to find in the art, craft and design areas, but jobs outside this field can also provide information and experience shared by businesses. This would allow you to make essential comparisons and judgements which link them with the business and professional practice unit. For example, health and safety legislation applies to all businesses. A comparison can therefore be made between working in a supermarket stacking shelves and handling and storing materials in an art, craft or design company.

This work may also give you ideas for creative work for other assignments: redesigning the supermarket logo and house style; designing advertisements to promote a product or service; creating fashions for a company uniform, and so on.

Collecting evidence from other sources

There are many opportunities for gathering further evidence for this unit. Local libraries, careers offices, local business directories and business enterprise bureaux are just some places where you can obtain extra information.

Trade fairs and exhibitions will provide you with a lot of evidence. Often they have stands which not only demonstrate the particular products or services of each industry but also illustrate the training and career paths that can be followed. For example, the annual BBC Clothes Show Live exhibition always has hundreds of stands, catwalks, demonstrations and merchandising outlets, as well as representations from many colleges offering fashion-related courses. There are often talks by top fashion designers on a variety of interesting and pertinent topics. A visit to a show like this, or to other large craft fairs, graphic materials suppliers' shows and major art exhibitions, could provide you with sufficient material to write an illustrated and word-processed report on some aspect of that industry. This would not only show evidence for the business and professional practice unit, but also cover the criteria and evidence for the core skills of Communication and Information Technology.

There are many opportunities for you to supplement evidence for this unit. It is a matter of being observant and recognising them as they occur. Anything can be used if it provides you with knowledge and understanding of professional practice and helps the progression of your own personal work in the field of art, craft and design.

Combining 2-D and 3-D ideas

Progression routes for careers and higher education

Which way?

During the course of your investigations you will have researched a variety of art, craft and design businesses and may have completed an industrial placement. You should now be aware of the vast range of employment opportunities in this area and may be wondering where you fit in.

▶ How do you see your future after GNVQ?

▶ What do you want to do for a job?

▶ Do you see yourself as a technician, a designer, an administrator or a maker?

Now is the time to think about which route you will need to take to reach your goal.

Employment routes directly from Advanced level GNVQ

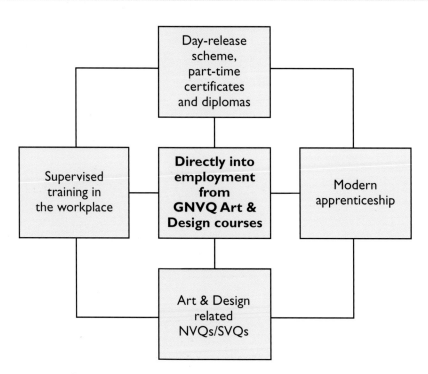

Progression routes for students going directly into employment

▶ Do you intend to look for work in your locality?

▶ Will you be living at home?

If this is your intention, you need to find out what is available. Visit the local job centre or the careers officer in your school or college. Look in trade journals and newspaper appointments sections.

▶ Are you interested in a job in art, craft or design?

A job in the field of **art** would be one where personal creativity and expression are uppermost. For example, a professional sculptor might be looking for a studio assistant to help with the preparation of forms for casting and be willing to teach the rudiments of the business to a keen student.

A **craft-based** job would involve work in which the relationship between materials and tools is used to develop objects. Craftworkers are usually involved in the whole process from start to finish. For example, a partnership producing tie-dye shirts might need someone to help dye the material and ensure quality control of the dying process in short-run batch production.

A job in the **design** area would be in a business where client-based requirements are the priority. As well as imaginative responses using creative thinking and innovative use of materials, the constraints of function, aesthetics, costs, ethics, production, marketability, time and resources play important roles. For example, a local company that designs and makes a range of children's toys and games might need someone to assist in conducting market research to develop the range.

Of course, you may find in these preliminary investigations that the job you would like to do after completing the GNVQ course cannot be obtained without some further training. How can you acquire more skills?

Further training through the workplace

Some companies run their own training schemes. This may involve:

▶ training by a supervisor in the company
▶ day release to college one day a week to learn both practical and theoretical skills
▶ an apprenticeship – this binds you to an employer while learning the necessary skills and competences of the job.

National and Scottish Vocational Qualifications (NVQs and SVQs)

These routes may lead to the nationally recognised NVQ and SVQ qualifications. This is a work-based qualification used by all industries. Each industrial lead body or training board has developed standards for NVQs/SVQs for their particular industry. For example, the Association for Ceramic Training Development (ACTD) is a lead body which has set standards in:

▶ decorating ceramic items (automotive)
▶ decorating ceramic items (non-automotive)
▶ firing ceramic items
▶ forming ceramic items (automotive)
▶ forming ceramic items (non-automotive).

Employees in these areas can therefore gain specific NVQs/SVQs for the jobs they do. In England and Wales, NVQs, as with GNVQs, are accredited by the National Council for Vocational Qualifications (NCVQ) – an umbrella organisation which approves standards for all vocational qualifications. In Scotland, SVQs are accredited by SCOTVEC, the Scottish Vocational

Educational Council. These qualifications are increasingly being taken up by industry, as they certify that a person is competent to perform a specified range of work-related tasks.

As you now understand the structure of a GNVQ course, you could start to think about taking an NVQ/SVQ. The GNVQ aims to give you a broad and wide-ranging (general) view of art, craft and design industries. NVQs/SVQs are awarded for the competences you can demonstrate related to a job in the art, craft or design workplace. They are concerned with what you can actually do, not just what you know in theory.

Like the GNVQ, NVQs/SVQs are available at different levels. They can be taken at whatever level you and your employer decide is the most appropriate at the time. The structure of the units and the method of assessment is similar to that used for the GNVQ. However, there are no grading criteria in NVQs (in GNVQs the grading criteria is between Pass, Merit and Distinction) – a candidate is either competent or not. The emphasis is on demonstrating that you can ably perform workplace tasks. Depending on the NVQ, you may also be asked to complete projects, assignments, a portfolio or written tests.

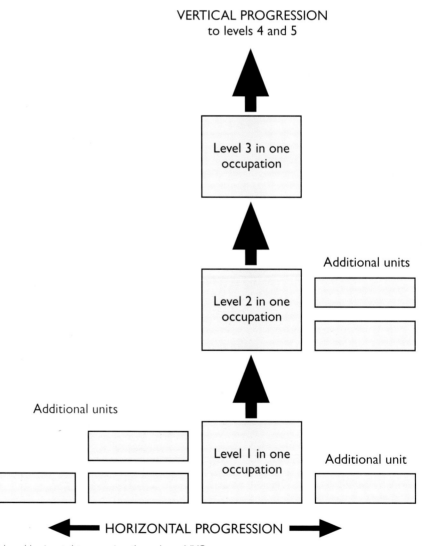

Vertical and horizontal progression through an NVQ

The central vertical column shows progression to other NVQ levels in the chosen area of employment. The additional units are achieved by taking NVQs from other related occupations.

It is also possible that one type of NVQ qualification will lead to further qualifications being achieved, some of which may be additional units from other work-related areas. This is called horizontal progression. For example, imagine you are working in the machine shop of a company producing decorative ceramic tiles and have achieved a level 2 NVQ in forming ceramic items (automotive). This is about showing competence in making and forming tiles using machines. You could add to this qualification by working for level 2 in forming ceramic items (non-automotive), which would be concerned with making and forming work by hand. If you were later moved into an area which demanded engineering and maintenance, you could add an engineering level 2 NVQ to your ceramic qualification.

Progression routes through further and higher education

Of course, there are other routes that you might follow into employment. These often involve taking further and higher education courses, and here the choice is wide and very varied. Most careers in art, craft and design are drawn from graduates of degree and HND courses. Usually large numbers of students apply for these courses and competition for places is vigorous. If you do not succeed in progressing directly to higher education, or want an extra year to develop your skills, then further education – a Foundation course in art and design – might be the answer.

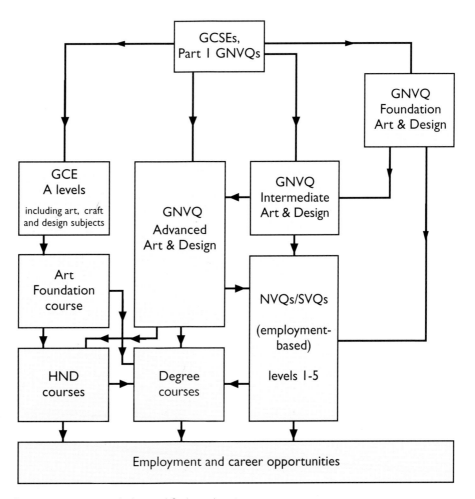

Progression routes into higher and further education

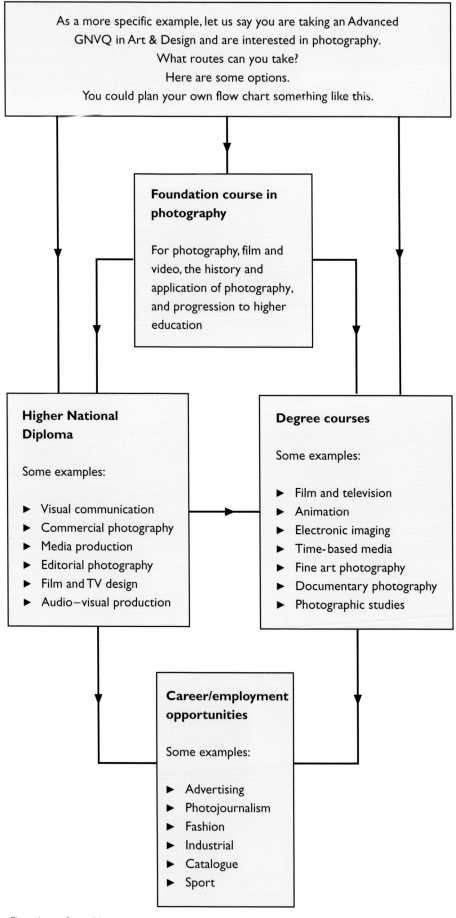

As a more specific example, let us say you are taking an Advanced GNVQ in Art & Design and are interested in photography.
What routes can you take?
Here are some options.
You could plan your own flow chart something like this.

Foundation course in photography

For photography, film and video, the history and application of photography, and progression to higher education

Higher National Diploma

Some examples:

► Visual communication
► Commercial photography
► Media production
► Editorial photography
► Film and TV design
► Audio–visual production

Degree courses

Some examples:

► Film and television
► Animation
► Electronic imaging
► Time-based media
► Fine art photography
► Documentary photography
► Photographic studies

Career/employment opportunities

Some examples:

► Advertising
► Photojournalism
► Fashion
► Industrial
► Catalogue
► Sport

Flow chart of possible progression routes

What courses are available?

Here is a selection of the vast range of courses that can be found under the umbrella of art, craft and design. We have grouped them together in areas of interest.

3-D studies

Museum & Exhibition Design
  BA (Hons)
Workshop or Studio Ceramics
  BA (Hons)
Wood, Metal & Plastics BA (Hons)
Industrial Modelmaking HND
Three-dimensional Design
  BA (Hons)
Furniture Making & Restoration
  HND
3-D Public Art & Crafts HND

Fine art

Painting BA (Hons)
Sculpture BA (Hons)
Print-making BA (Hons)

Architecture

3-D Design: Interior Architecture
  BA (Hons)
Building Design HND
Architecture BA (Hons)
Architectural Glass HND
Architectural Lettering, Heraldry &
  Calligraphy HND
Architectural Stained Glass HND/
  BA (Hons)

Fashion

Fashion Design for the European
  Market HND
Textile for Fashion HND
Fashion & Textile Design BA (Hons)
Design (Fashion & Fashion
  Marketing) HND
Fashion Design Technology
  BA (Hons)
Knitwear Design & Practice
  BSc (Hons)
Fashion/Surface Pattern: Fashion
  Option HND
Footwear Fashion & Technology
  HND
Product development for the
  Fashion Industries BA (Hons)
Fashion Styling BA (Hons)
Menswear BA (Hons)

Textiles

Woven & Printed Textiles
  BA (Hons)
Textiles & Fibres HND/BA (Hons)
Textile Design HND
Fashion & Textile Design BA (Hons)
Clothing Technology HND
Textile & Surface Pattern HND
Knitwear Design & Production
  BSc (Hons)
Constructed Textiles BSC (Hons)
Printed Textiles BA (Hons)
(European) Textile Design
  BA (Hons)

Crafts

Design: Crafts (3-D Option) HND
Design & Crafts for the
  Entertainment Industries HND
Art & Craft Studies BA (Hons)
Design Crafts (Creative Bookbinding
  & Printmaking) HND
Historic Decorative Crafts HND
Jewellery and Metalwork BA (Hons)
Design Crafts (Blacksmithing) HND
Silversmithing, Jewellery & Allied
  Crafts BA (Hons)
Ceramics with Glass BA (Hons)
Furniture Design & Craftsmanship
  BA (Hons)

Design

Design for Industry BSc (Hons)
Packaging Design HND
Graphic Design HND
Design (Visual Communication)
  HND
Illustration BA (Hons)
Industrial Design HND/BA (Hons)
Graphic Design & Advertising
  BA (Hons)
Electronic Design BSc (Hons)
Design (Product Design) HND
Interior Design HND
Design: Technical & Natural History
  Illustration HND
Design Management BA (Hons)

Design: Illustration & Printmaking
  BA (Hons)
Information Illustration HND
Design for Floorcoverings & Interior
  Textiles BA (Hons)

Computing

Software Systems for the Arts &
  Media BSc (Hons)
Electronic Media & Reprography
  HND
Animation & Electronic Media
  BA (Hons)
Typographic Design HND
Design & Technology of Video
  Games BA (Hons)
Newspaper Design & Infographics
  HND
Design: Multidisciplinary Computer
  Applications HND

Theatre

Theatre Studies (Design) BA (Hons)
Theatre & Media Production HND
Technical Theatre Arts BA (Hons)
Costume for the Stage & Screen
  BA (Hons)
Costume Design & Wardrobe
  BA (Hons)
Theatre with Visual Practice BA (Hons)

Media

Documentary Production BA (Hons)
European Audio-Visual Promotion
  BA (Hons)
Art, Design & Media BA (Hons)
Professional Media (Graphic,
  Photographic, Video) BA (Hons)
Film & Television Production HND
Advertising (Copywriting & Art
  Direction) HND
Film & Photography BA (Hons)
Cultural & Media Studies BA (Hons)
Interactive & Broadcast Media
  BA (Hons)
Design: Television Operation HND
Design: Arts & Event Administration
  HND

Applying for places on higher education courses

Researching choices

If you have not already done so, you will soon have to come to some conclusions about your own direction. For those students who want to progress into higher education and, in particular, onto degree or HND courses, the question is often 'Where do I start?'

Before thinking about which course you would like to take, make sure you have sufficient commitment and enthusiasm to see it through. Recent surveys show that, of the whole student population, one in ten drop out of courses by the end of the first year. You must be sure this is not going to happen to you.

If you decide to go ahead, think about the type of course that is right for you. Should you take a degree, or is a Higher National Diploma or a diploma in higher education a better choice for what you want to do? Don't be prejudiced, find out about the differences and choose the most appropriate one.

Think:

▶ What am I good at?
▶ What do I like doing?
▶ What am I capable of?
▶ Where would I like to be (close to/far from home; small/large college; urban/rural area)?

Be aware of the full range of opportunities available within the art, craft and design context. Consider broader progression routes rather than just the often oversubscribed popular ones.

Sources of information for courses

One of the most up-to-date sources of information on courses is **ECCTIS 2000**. This is a national database of college and university courses held on computer. Many schools, colleges and local careers offices use it. It will provide full details on courses that match your needs, as well as entry requirements and course content.

A new edition of ECCTIS is now available called **ECCTIS+**. This, in addition to providing information on 100,000 courses, gives a wide range of related careers information and will help you to choose exactly the right course for your circumstances.

Two publications provide valuable information. The **UCAS Handbook** lists all the college courses, their content and the relevant entry requirements. The **GATE Directory** (GNVQ Access to Higher Education) – a UCAS/NCVQ publication – is a useful guide for GNVQ students, as it lists all the college courses relevant to direct progression from GNVQ courses.

You will find it helpful to write to individual colleges for prospectuses, which will give full details of courses on offer and describe the college location and environment. If you want a selection of these, **The Prospectus Delivery Service** will dispatch them to your school or college. This mailing service is operated by HEIST (The Higher Education Information Services Trust) and

UCAS, and is free to school and college students during term-time. There is a charge for delivery direct to your home. For more information about this service write to The Prospectus Delivery Service, c/o MailLin, Bellamy Road, Mansfield, Nottinghamshire NG18 4LN.

School, college and careers libraries have books, magazines and pamphlets from a number of sources with up-to-the-minute information on courses and career guidance. They also have specialist books on different areas of art and design.

When you have digested all the information and read all the prospectuses, try to visit as many of the colleges that interest you as possible. Prepare questions that you would like answered on the day. The majority of colleges run open days or pre-taster courses. Use them – forming a first-hand impression is far better than simply reading about it, and talking to existing students on a course will often provide a different viewpoint than you would otherwise get.

Nearer home, careers services often organise local conventions or conferences on career opportunities and higher education progression. These provide the opportunity to talk to representatives from colleges and industry, both locally and nationally, who will provide information and answer your questions on courses and career paths.

Remember, all of this is about your future. Help yourself by getting as much assistance and advice as you can. This is a big decision. **Be positive, practical and professional.**

The process of applying

In the past, art, craft and design students have used the specialised Art and Design Admissions Registry (ADAR) to apply for their courses. From September 1996, ADAR merges with UCAS (Universities and Colleges Admissions Service). There will now be only one application system, although for art students there are two routes with two distinct deadline dates. Your tutors will have more information and will help when the time comes to fill in your application form.

Make sure you have all your qualifications to hand, ready to enter them onto the qualifications page. You will need to know:

- the GNVQ centre number, name and address
- the GNVQ programme title (this should be underlined)
- the full list of units
  - mandatory (man)
  - optional (op)
  - key skills (ks)
- unit tests (ut) achieved, where applicable
- additional studies
  - extra GNVQ units (add)
  - number of additional units (in brackets)
  - GCE A level(s), AS level(s)
  - NVQ/SVQ units.

Preparing a personal statement

In addition to this factual information, you are required to provide a personal statement. Your tutors will write a reference which will give the admissions registrars information about your all-round abilities and character. The statement you have to prepare is *your* case for entry to a particular course. You must give clear reasons why you are making the application. Admissions tutors will be looking for potential and the ability to express ideas. Concisely written information, using competent communication skills, will give a good impression.

There are several helpful starting points for this section of the form:

▶ your National Record of Achievement which will indicate strengths worth emphasising
▶ your GNVQ portfolio with its summaries and evaluations of objectives achieved
▶ references from recent employers – industrial placements, part-time jobs, weekend work, and so on
▶ your school or college tutors and advisers.

Remember, do not just write about what you are doing at the moment – try to analyse and relate it to what you hope to get from a higher level of study. Your personal statement should therefore include:

▶ a positive link to the area of study
▶ the background to that link
▶ how any voluntary work recently undertaken has links with your choice of course
▶ other interests and relevant hobbies
▶ how key skills are relevant to the course
▶ your career plans.

Preparing a portfolio for interview

Get it right!

Your UCAS form is the only thing that the admissions tutor sees when deciding whether to offer you an interview for a course. Therefore, it is essential that you take time and care in getting it right. Practise on a blank form first – a good idea is to make one or two photocopies of the form and practise on them. You are an art student, so presentation is important. Check that you can fill the spaces properly and choose a good paragraph style for your statement. Make sure that the information you present is truthful – you may have to talk about what you have written to someone who is an expert in the field. Avoid crossing out words and do not use correction fluids.

Treat the form like a job application. It is your opportunity to sell yourself and to persuade the admissions tutor that you are right for the course. It is worth spending some time over its completion. Don't leave it until the last minute – admissions tutors do not wait until the deadline before sending out invitations for interviews.

Remember All this work is part of Element 5.3 of the business and professional practice unit. Evidence has to be provided which shows that you can produce personal information to pursue progression opportunities.

The range of evidence includes letters of application, a CV, **filling in application forms** and **producing a personal statement**. All this has to be completed within quite strict time limits and therefore it is best if you set a timescale for what can be a lengthy process. Don't leave it too late – your future might be at stake. The following chart gives you some indication of the process and timescale of making an application.

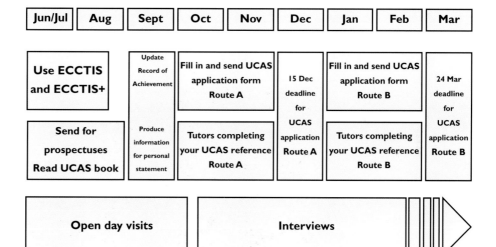

Chart showing timescale of applying for a place in higher education

activity **23**   **Research and map out a personal career plan.**

WHAT TO DO ...

Using the chart on page 74, fill in the relevant details as instructed. This will give you the opportunity to outline two or three prospective career routes. They are obviously not firm proposals at this time, but they will give you an indication of possible ways you might want to go, and the exercise could be repeated later when you are more certain. ...

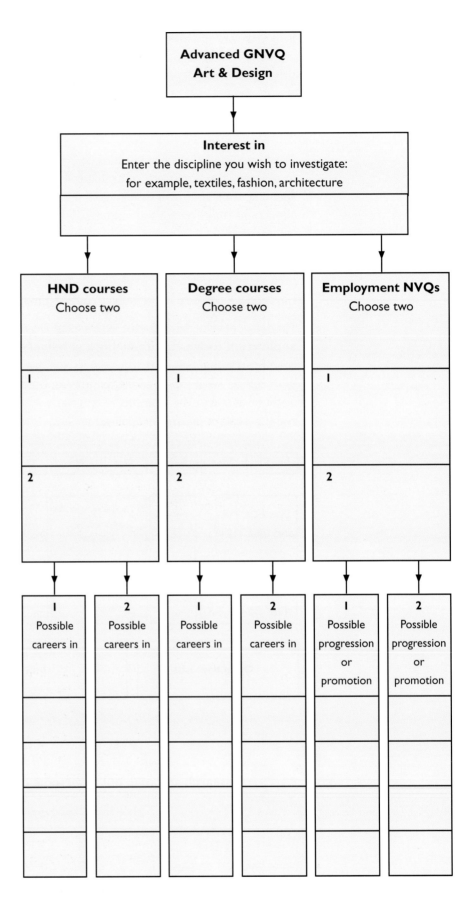

Advanced GNVQ
Art & Design

Interest in
Enter the discipline you wish to investigate:
for example, textiles, fashion, architecture

HND courses Choose two	**Degree courses** Choose two	**Employment NVQs** Choose two
1	1	1
2	2	2

1 Possible careers in	2 Possible careers in	1 Possible careers in	2 Possible careers in	1 Possible progression or promotion	2 Possible progression or promotion

You will need to refer to the UCAS book, college prospectuses and any other
information in order to fill this chart in correctly

Your career plan

Appendix 1
Activities checklist

This section lists all the activities in the book. Tick them off as you complete them. There is a column for you to add a completion date, and a column for you to enter other mandatory units or practical work to which the activity might link.

You are not expected to do all the activities.

If you choose to fulfil the unit using only:

▶ **comparative research**, complete all the activities in the Introduction and Chapters 1 and 5.
▶ a **simulated business**, complete all the activities in the Introduction and Chapters 2 and 5.
▶ an **industrial placement**, complete all the activities in the Introduction and Chapters 3 and 5.

If you are going to use an **integrated approach**, select all the relevant activities which help you to gather the evidence for the business and professional practice unit.

Check the evidence indicators for this unit to make sure you know what you have to produce.

Activity	Chapter	Page	Activity	Links with	Date completed
1	Intro	4	Find out about product and service industries in art, craft and design in your area.		
2	1	12	Devise a questionnaire which will help you to discover different types of businesses, their form of ownership and their aims and objectives.		
3	1	15	Investigate the business resources and facilities of a local company.		
4	1	15	Investigate two local art, craft or design businesses to discover how their demand has been established and fulfilled.		

Activity	Chapter	Page	Activity	Links with	Date completed
5	1	19	Find out from local art, craft and design businesses whether they conduct market research and, if so, how they do it.		
6	1	20	Carry out your own market research. Compile a questionnaire for local distribution which aims to collect public opinion on an art, craft or design product or service.		
7	1	22	Choose two art, craft or design-based companies and explain how they conform to different parts of the regulations covering responsibilities to clients.		
8	1	24	Either (a) use a local artist, craftworker or designer and investigate how their codes of practice influence the work they produce, or (b) compile a report about professional codes of practice in one particular art, craft or design-based industry.		
9	1	27	Select an art, craft or design business and, choosing health and safety and at least one other section, make a report on what you would do to ensure that proper legal obligations are carried out.		
10	2	30	Investigate areas which may have potential for an art, craft or design business and draw up an action plan.		
11	2	33	Form a discussion group to talk about physical, human and financial resources and their implications for the chosen simulated business. Make a list of all the resources that may be needed under appropriate headings.		

Advanced GNVQ Art & Design

Activity	Chapter	Page	Activity	Links with	Date completed
12	2	40	Within the group, decide who is going to be responsible for each of the following business functions: planning, administration, accountancy, research and development, production, marketing and selling. Write a report. Distribute it to the members. Speak to the meeting.		
13	2	41	Produce the goods (small batch of items) or provide the service for the business simulation.		
14	2	43	Make a display of your work. Include the product or service offered, together with reports, notes, diagrams, sketches, photographs, graphs and charts which clearly indicate the business potential, opportunity and professional practices that have been carried out.		
15	3	51	Draw maps which show where the industrial placement company is sited in (a) the locality and (b) the neighbourhood.		
16	3	51	Draw a detailed plan of the business premises. Include notes which explain the reasons for the layout and indicate the number of employees working in each area.		
17	3	52	Investigate as many of the listed business functions in your industrial placement as you can. You may discover that the company places more importance on some of them. List them in order of the company's priority and make notes about the reasons for their importance.		

Activity	Chapter	Page	Activity	Links with	Date completed
18	3	53	In your work placement, investigate and write a report on the following three operations: (a) a creative role; (b) a technical support role; and (c) an administrative service role.		
19	3	56	Ask if you can do some work-shadowing for a day. From your notes and observations, write a report about 'a day in the life of . . .' (fill in the designated job).		
20	3	57	Investigate (a) health and safety regulations, and (b) one other statutory requirement that must be observed by your industrial placement business. Write a report on the results of your investigation.		
21	3	57	Investigate up to three different career opportunities offered by your industrial placement business. In particular, research the qualifications, courses and time needed to qualify for these careers.		
22	3	58	Either (a) write a full report on what you have discovered about business and professional practices in your industrial placement, or (b) write a report, in diary form, of your own day-to-day activities during the industrial placement.		
23	5	73	Research and map out a personal career plan.		

Appendix 2
Unit specification checklist

The specifications for each element of the business and professional practice unit are listed in the charts on pages 80–2. Beside each performance criterion there is a series of boxes which show you where specific evidence can be obtained from the investigations, research and work produced using this book. All you have to do is:

- ▶ check which activity you have completed
- ▶ find the corresponding box which contains that activity number or related work
- ▶ Tick the small box below it.

Some activities and related work cover a lot more than just a single box, so look carefully through them when you are checking which ones to fill in.

Where possible, your aim should be to fill in at least two boxes against every performance criterion. When you have done this, you will have produced most of the evidence needed to successfully complete this unit.

Check against the evidence indicators for each element to make sure you have not forgotten anything.

Remember that you have been working in an integrated way. This means that you can separate and record evidence from many sources in the work you have produced.

GNVQ Art & Design activities

Element 5.1: Investigate business practice in art, craft and design

Performance criteria	Evidence				
1 Identify and give examples of different types of businesses	Intro. p. 4 **Act. 1**	Ch. 1 p. 12 **Act. 2**	Ch. 2 p. 30 **Act. 10**	Ch. 2 p. 41 **Act. 13**	Ch. 3 p. 55 **quest.**
2 Describe the aims and objectives of different types of businesses	Ch. 1 p. 12 **Act. 2**	Ch. 1 p. 19 **Act. 5**	Ch. 2 p. 41 **Act. 13**	Ch. 3 p. 51 **Act. 16**	Ch. 3 p. 55 **quest.**
3 Describe the functions and resources required in business	Ch. 1 p. 15 **Act. 3**	Ch. 2 p. 33 **Act. 11**	Ch. 2 p. 40 **Act. 12**	Ch. 3 p. 51 **Act. 15**	Ch. 3 p. 52 **Act. 17**
4 Identify clients of art, craft and design	Ch. 1 p. 15 **Act. 3**	Ch. 1 p. 15 **Act. 4**	Ch. 1 p. 20 **Act. 6**	Ch. 3 p. 55 **quest.**	
5 Identify the demand for art, craft and design products and services	Ch. 1 p. 15 **Act. 4**	Ch. 2 p. 30 **Act. 10**	Ch. 2 p. 41 **Act. 13**	Ch. 3 p. 55 **quest.**	
6 Describe art, craft and design business practices	Ch. 2 p. 40 **Act. 12**	Ch. 2 p. 43 **Act. 14**	Ch. 3 p. 51 **Act. 16**	Ch. 3 p. 56 **Act. 19**	

Intro. = Introduction   Ch. = chapter   p. = page   Act. = activity   quest. = questionnaire

1 Check which activity you have completed.
2 Find the corresponding box which contains that activity number or related work.
3 Tick the small box below it.

Evidence indicators

▶ Investigative report on the sector, covering the range for types of business, with an example of each type. Aims and related objectives should be given for each example.

▶ Two case studies drawn from an in-depth investigation of art, craft and design business practice. The case studies should be based on research into one example of a commercial business and one example of a public service or a voluntary business. They should include details of business functions carried out, resources used, demand identified and business practices involved. If the two case studies do not cover all the requirements of the range, supplementary evidence may need to be provided in the form of notes.

Element 5.2: Analyse professional responsibilities in art, craft and design

Performance criteria	Evidence			
1 Explain the ways in which organisations' and professional bodies' codes of practice seek to influence art, craft and design	Ch. 1 p. 24 **Act. 8**	Ch. 3 p. 58 **Act. 22**	Ch. 3 p. 55 **quest.**	
2 Describe the work responsibilities and practices of artists, craftspeople and designers	Ch. 1 p. 27 **Act. 9**	Ch. 3 p. 53 **Act. 18**	Ch. 3 p. 56 **Act. 19**	Ch. 3 p. 58 **Act. 22**
3 Describe the influence of legislation on work responsibilities and practice	Ch. 1 p. 27 **Act. 9**	Ch. 2 p. 39 **resp.**	Ch. 3 p. 57 **Act. 20**	Ch. 3 p. 58 **Act. 22**
4 Explain the importance of meeting responsibilities to clients	Ch. 1 p. 22 **Act. 7**	Ch. 2 p. 41 **Act. 13**	Ch. 3 p. 58 **Act. 22**	
5 Carry out and record professional work practices in simulated situations	Ch. 2 p. 40 **Act. 12**	Ch. 2 p. 41 **Act. 13**	Ch. 2 p. 43 **Act. 14**	

Ch. = chapter   p. = page   Act. = activity   quest. = questionnaire   resp. = professional responsibilities

1 Check which activity you have completed.
2 Find the corresponding box which contains that activity number or related work.
3 Tick the small box below it.

Evidence indicators

▶ Investigative report covering the range for organisations, professional bodies and legislation.
▶ Two case studies based on in-depth investigation of professional practice, including details of work responsibilities and practices drawn from more than one of the following contexts: art, craft, design.

Element 5.3: Investigate progression opportunities and develop related skills

Performance criteria	Evidence	
1 Describe skills and qualifications required for different areas of employment	Ch. 3 p. 57 **Act. 21**	Ch. 5 p. 73 **Act. 23**
2 Identify progression routes leading to different qualifications and areas of employment	Ch. 3 p. 57 **Act. 21**	Ch. 5 p. 73 **Act. 23**
3 Evaluate own suitability for progression routes	Ch. 5 pp. 64–6 **routes**	Ch. 5 pp. 67–9 **app.**
4 Demonstrate skills relating to pursuit of progression opportunities	Ch. 5 pp. 70–1 **app./PS**	Ch. 5 p. 73 **Act. 23**
5 Produce personal information to pursue progression opportunities employment	Ch. 5 pp. 71–3 **PS**	Ch. 5 p. 73 **Act. 23**

Ch. = chapter   p. = page   Act. = activity   routes = progression routes   app. = applying
PS = personal statement

1 Check which activity you have completed.
2 Find the corresponding box which contains that activity number or related work.
3 Tick the small box below it.

Evidence indicators

▶ Report outlining the typical skills and qualifications required for the areas of employment ranged.
▶ Studies of two jobs in different areas of employment. Each study should identify at least two progression routes and evaluate the student's suitability for the job.
▶ Record of observation by the assessor of the student demonstrating interview and telephone skills in at least two situations.
▶ Two examples of each type of personal information in the range.

Index